I
Was Never
Alone
Amen

ANNE HAYES

ISBN 978-1-64458-927-4 (paperback)
ISBN 978-1-64458-928-1 (digital)

Christian Faith Publishing, Inc.
832 Park Avenue
Meadville, PA 16335
www.christianfaithpublishing.com

Printed in the United States of America

T his book is dedicated to those who have not been seen, heard, loved, nor felt safe. This is a journey of a simple woman who had no support, no mentors, no one to watch her back and put herself at the mercy of cruel and self-centered loved ones.

This book is a testimony of a woman who trusted in God and, as a result, lived a supernatural life full of miracles, enlightenment, and direction. God has given me the courage to write this book so that you know, when faced with extreme adversity, you can get to the other side and live the life you were intended to live.

> We must be willing to let go of the life we planned
> so as to have the life that is waiting for us.
> —Joseph Campbell

I hope my journey will awaken you to your journey and inspire you to take the first small step to becoming free to be you and discover your true destiny.

CHAPTER 1

Pop Goes the Weasel

Where to start the journey was a conundrum. I felt I needed to capture your attention so you would not put this book down. Again, the egotistic mind needing applause, admiration, and recognition for a job well done. Fiddlesticks! How about plain, down to earth, unpretentious honesty. So here goes.

I was around two years old. I was living in Bangor, North Wales. No more diapers for me, I was a big girl now; I wore panties. So like any other morning, I slid down the stairs, bright-eyed and bushy tailed. I went to find my mommy. As usual, she would give me this disgusting white stuff to drink in a glass. I was a very fussy eater; in fact, I did not like eating at all, which put my parents in a state of paranoia, and their life mission was to force food down my mouth no matter what. They were totally convinced I would simply die of starvation and that would simply be the end of little Anne. The doctor thought they were crazy, and as I grew older, it slowly became apparent they had the most bizarre idiosyncrasies.

I don't ever remember my father being present at breakfast. He would leave early for work, so I presumed, and had not returned by the time I was ready for bed.

After breakfast, it was time for me to get dressed. On the ground floor, you could enter each room in a circular pattern. I would run around and around, hopping on one leg through the doorways. What an adventure; it had no end. I imagined being in a race with other children and I was ahead of them all. I was the roadrunner, see me go! No one could catch me. I was invincible.

My mother would dress me in front of the fireplace in the living room. First, my big girl panties. *Oh no, I cannot get my foot through the right leg.* I simply wasn't trying hard enough. Groaning, pushing, it wasn't happening. My mother was laughing hysterically. What was going on? My mother had sewn one of my underwear legs up at the request of my father because it was April Fool's Day. I remember my whole body starting to burn up like a volcano. I was furious. I don't think I cried. I just screamed noises of frustration and disgust. "How could you do this to me?"

She showed no signs of remorse. I think I ran upstairs to my bedroom.

I don't remember much about the daily activities of my childhood, but there are some events embedded in my memory.

One vivid memory was when I started school. I was four years old when I first attended my first day at school, and I was terrified. I cried hysterically and refused to walk down the hill to school. So my codependent mother would carry me all the way there. I would take my little white stuffed lamb with me and would continually cry all over it during class. I was extremely traumatized being separated from my mother. They called it separation anxiety. I was scared I was not safe and felt impending doom.

On the way home from school, I remember skipping up the hill, feeling a sense of relief. "I wasn't carried off by the wicked witch that lived behind the classroom walls!" She waited there patiently, waiting for the precise time to devour little children like me.

On one occasion, on my way home from school, I found a large colorful bead. I knew for certain it was the lost crystal from the crown of a beautiful princess who was being kept against her will in an old abandoned castle. She had managed to remove a crystal from her crown. She desperately threw the crystal out of the window hoping someone somewhere would find it and come searching for her. I kept that priceless jewel under my pillow. Her dilemma was now brought to light. I would plan carefully how to execute my strategy, to be her hero and save the day.

Another vivid memory, around five years old, was playing in my blowup swimming pool in the front yard. I would play for hours, running in and out of it, splashing and feeling free as a butterfly. I lived in an imaginary world. I was center stage and I was a swimmer and a dancer extraordinaire. Then all of a sudden, I would stop what I was doing, stand still, and be overcome with excitement, so much so I had to tell my parents about this newfound wonderland. Dripping with water from head to toe, I ran frantically to the backdoor. As I turned the corner to enter the backdoor, I slipped ever so gracefully and crashed through the glass plane of an adjoining door. My whole body went through the glass to my utter dismay. My parents rushed to my rescue, making sure I was alright and that I had not badly cut myself.

One or two days later, the glass pane was replaced. Everything was back in order. Ah, thank goodness for that.

Every weekend during the summer, I played on the front lawn in my rubber swimming pool. The water was cold and refreshing. I played to my heart's content. I had no recollection of time. I would work my way up to a state of unbelievable ecstasy. Then, almost momentarily, I would stop and say, "I just simply must share this excitement with my mum and dad."

Off I dashed, running as fast as I could, almost there, coming to the last turn. Oh no, moment of deja vu—straight through the glass. Hurray, through the pane with no cuts! I slid like a pro. This was becoming fun. My mom and dad came running, but this time they were not too pleased.

Again a few days later, the pane of glass was replaced. Everything looked in order once again.

From about eighteen months to five years old, we lived in North Wales. Except for school, I liked living there. I had a friend called Paul who lived three or four houses down from where I lived. We would play, but I don't remember exactly what we did; those memories are vague. I guess we did not do anything memorable or it would be vivid in my mind.

I do remember visiting Mr. Philips down the road. I would walk down the street to his house all by myself. When I reached his gate,

I paused and slowly opened the old grey dilapidated gate. It was not much taller than me. Oh boy, once I walked through the gate, I entered another world, a place where only fairies lived.

In his front and backyard were the most beautiful trees and flowers. There was a water fountain that made the most enchanting noise, and the fairies would dance and sing. Their dresses looked like delicate silk flowing in the wind. Blue, purple, yellow, all the colors of the rainbow. Their tiny porcelain-like faces would glow like the morning sun. I had to hide behind the large oak tree, trying to stick my neck out in a contorted fashion so I could observe them secretly. Why, if they knew I was there observing them, they would run and hide, and that would never do! After watching the fairies ever so closely, I decided it was time to go find my friend.

"Mr. Philips, Mr. Philips, it's Anne, are you there?" I did not really need to call him because he was almost always in his tomato shed. He grew prize tomatoes. They were redder, juicier, and larger than any tomato I had ever seen.

He came out of his shed with great enthusiasm, overjoyed to see me. His wife had died a few years back, and I guess he was lonely. "Come over here, Anne, let's measure you." He would put me at the back of the shed's door and mark off my height. It was great fun to see the amount I had grown. I was very tall for my age.

Mr. Philips was average height, slightly overweight. He always wore his straw hat. The wear and tear of the hat showed he was an avid gardener and had spent many hours outside gardening to his heart's content. His face was wrinkled and old, but when he smiled, he lit up the world. His smile would stretch from ear to ear. His hair was salt and pepper in color and would stick out of his hat like a scarecrow. He wore brown overalls and heavy boots. I am not surprised the fairies loved him; what was there not to love?

We talked in the garden for a while, and then we went into the house. We went into the front room where all the formal furniture was. I would have the privilege of sitting in the formal chair. It was heavily embroidered, had wooden arms, and when I sat on it, my feet did not reach the floor. Mr. Philips would give me a cold refreshing drink, usually orange juice, and a chocolate biscuit. I felt really special.

Then the moment I had been waiting for—Mr. Philips had a wooden windmill. I held my breath with great anticipation, watching him move the wings of the windmill around and around clockwise. As soon as he stopped, the most delightful tune would play. I was totally mesmerized watching the wings move around and around. The tune took me to a far-off land where children were playing on a merry-go-round, their hair blowing in the wind. They were laughing at the sheer delight of feeling free. There were beautiful monarch butterflies flying everywhere. I truly wished I could be there, because I too was lonely at times. I had no one to really play with. So something or someone out there made sure me and Mr. Philips became great pals, and there was never a dull moment. Both of us escaped reality if only for a short time. The song the windmill played was called "Tulips of Amsterdam."

I finally decided it was time to go home. I didn't want my mother to worry about me. I gave my old friend a giant teddy bear hug and wished him well until I returned again. He looked happy and content. He continued to wave to me as I walked up the road to my house until I disappeared out of sight.

When I got home, my dinner was ready. Dover sole, mashed potatoes, and peas. I told you I was a picky eater, so because I refused to eat anything other than fish, my mother gave me the same meal every day for three years. Yes you heard me right—Dover sole, mashed potatoes, and peas every day for three years! I always ate by myself. I never thought it was odd until I heard other children ate with their families. I don't ever remember my father being home during my younger years. Now looking back, no wonder Mr. Philips and myself were such good friends; each of us filled a void for each other.

As a child, I would always carry two special dolls around with me, Pinky and Perky. They were rubberized dolls. Pinky had black curly hair and a kind of smile that always welcomed me. She looked happy to see me when I picked her up. Perky, on the other hand, had blond curly hair and her smile was demure. Perky never left Pinky's side; they were inseparable. They wear the most beautiful clothes, all handmade by my mother. They wore bright colorful dresses with a matching coat and hat. They wore hand-knitted cardigans, all handmade by my mom. In fact, when they went out on the town, I don't think you could have found a better dressed, well color-coordinated pair of ladies.

I also had a wooden donkey. You could push him around the room like a pram (stroller in America). I would put Pinky and Perky on his back and take them for a ride. It was such great fun. I loved that donkey. As I grew older, I showed less interest in him. Then on one devastating day, my mom and dad gave my donkey away. I could hardly believe they could do such a thing without asking my permission. When I was young, I thought my parents could do no wrong. Alas, through the years, I learnt my feelings never counted.

I was told by my mother, later in life, that I went to visit Mrs. Wilkins, the neighbor behind our house, and made cookies with her. How strange I remembered every detail when I visited Mr. Philips but had no recollection of visiting Mrs. Wilkins. My mother told me when I was older that Mrs. Wilkins said, "Anne will never go anywhere with her brains, but her personality will take her far." No wonder she wasn't one of my favorite people.

When I lived in Bangor, I had a bunny rabbit called Snowy. She was white as snow and very soft and cuddly. She lived outside in a cage. I would bring her into the garage and play with her. She was not very entertaining. She just wiggled her nose. One evening, she peed on my beautiful pink nightdress and I was horrified. Like, she did it on purpose, right?

A few weeks later, they bought me a small white poodle. I called her Penny. That was more like it. I chased her, rolled the ball to her, she had the most beautiful white floppy ears, and she fit perfectly under my arm. I think I was "in love." She was my constant companion. I was no longer alone. That called for a celebration dance.

It is hard to believe when I was aged five that my parents were in their late thirties. They always appeared to be so old, they were practically never any fun. Although there was one occasion when my dad stepped up to the plate. We would kick a ball back and forth to each other. We would pretend we were playing football (soccer in America). It was unbelievably thrilling. I would get really excited on the weekend when my dad wanted to go into the backyard and kick the ball around. I guess ever since I was young, I had the ability to be in the moment and experience uncontrollable joy.

I remember this one particular afternoon when the sun was shining brightly. It was a breath of fresh air when it was sunny in the United Kingdom; the weather was usually overcast or raining. Dad was happy, an unusual event. He was always consumed with work. Time stood still, and you could actually hear laughter in the backyard. My mother was in her usual spot, in the kitchen doing something and looking out of the window.

I made the most amazing pass to my dad and he kicked it back to me ever so skillfully. My turn to show off my expert skills. I dribbled the ball and positioned myself in the exact precise position to kick a goal. Nothing was in my way. I pulled my foot back and then thrusted it forward to kick the ball toward the goal. My foot kicked the ball with power and determination. It flew through the air and went through the posts; yes! An amazing goal. Even my dad was impressed. "I am the champion, my friend, and I will fight to the end!"

Now it was my dad's turn. He moved his foot up to the ball, kicked with all his might. The ball flew through the air, but where was it going, not toward the goal posts. It flew right over my head and went straight to the front window in the lounge. *Oh no! Crash! Bang! Disaster!* This was definitely not good.

My mother came running out screaming, "Look what you have done!" Her face was red, and I think smoke was coming out of her ears. She looked straight at my dad with piercing eyes. She waited impatiently for his answer. I could not believe what he said.

"It wasn't me, it was Anne. She kicked the ball through the window!"

I screamed, "I didn't do that, it was you!"

He continued denying he was guilty of the crime. To tell you the truth, I was totally disgusted that a grown man, my father, had to blame a child for his action. Again the pane was replaced, everything back in place.

I would love to tell you that was the last pane of glass that had to be replaced in our house. But alas, I will spare you the details; yes, once again I was in my swimming pool, and yes, I went running to the backdoor. Do I need to say more?

I loved living in Bangor, North Wales, but I guess I had nothing else to compare it to. I was an only child and did not even wonder what it would be like having any siblings. It was easy for me to entertain myself and I lived in my world. I did not realize it was such an asset having such imagination that served me well the rest of my life.

Before I take you to the next phase of my journey, I simply have to tell you a couple more stories. When you are reading this book, I want you to identify with the feelings, emotions, and beliefs that were planted in my subconscious mind during the early stages of life.

Although I was happy living in my own world, I was not secure interacting in the real world. Remember my reaction when I started going to school for the first time?

I was told later in life by my father that when I was a baby, they took me with them on an outing. One night, they left me in my crib alone while they went out to dinner. I guess I woke up and became hysterical. When they eventually came back to the room, my father said I had taken the reading lamp off the table and completely pulled it apart. Its bare electrical wires were showing. If I had touched the wires, I would have died. I don't think it ever occurred to my parents they could have gone to prison. Again, was someone or something out there watching over me?

Going back to age five, I awoke one night in the house and was completely alone. I remember feeling terrified, running all over the house, calling for my mommy, but she was nowhere to be found. I remember very vividly opening a window in the living room and climbing out. The only thing I could think of doing was to run down the street to my friend's house. I started banging on their door, and when they opened it, my mother was there. The first thing she said was, "Don't tell you father." She did not feel it necessary to comfort me in any way. She did not reassure me that it was not going to happen again.

On a more pleasant note, I want to tell you how I developed my love for flowers. When it was my mother's birthday, my father would send her flowers. Not one bunch of flowers, but a dozen different types of flowers. The delivery man would bring in a cellophane bag, about four feet tall and three feet wide, and place it on the living room floor. From a little girl's point of view, it seemed like the fairies had worked all through the night, gathering all the different neon-colored flowers and carefully wrapped them in individual bright-colored paper and rainbow-colored ribbons. I was ecstatic, speechless, and extremely anxious to help unwrap the parcel and help my mother put the flowers in vases. I cannot remember my mother's reaction to the flowers, but I do remember she complained she did not have enough vases, and that irritated her.

So one day, my dad got a promotion with another company, and it was time for us to leave Bangor and move to Morecambe, England.

I never knew if I said goodbye to Mr. Philips. I really hope I hugged him and wished him well.

CHAPTER 2

Always Let Them Underestimate You

I don't remember traveling overnight to Morcambe or seeing the new house for the first time. It was a two-story house and there was a canal at the back. The house was full of light, not like the house in Bangor that was very dark. My bedroom was on the second floor, and I loved it. Everything seemed so fresh and inviting. I was very pleased and said to myself, "I am really going to enjoy living here."

We did not live far from the beach. My mother and I would take Penny for a walk once a week to the ocean. There was a certain path we took from the house to our destination. It involved crossing a railroad track. One day, I found an incredible treasure. A large English penny had been flattened on the track. It was gigantic, no doubt, it should have found its way to a treasure chest; instead, it went into my pocket and no one was going to take it. Remember, we are going back almost fifty years and the currency was very different then. The English penny was brown and very large.

After the railway track, we had to cross a field. My mother would take Penny's leash off, and Penny would spot a couple of sheep in the distance and run after them and disappear over the horizon. My mother would go into a complete meltdown, calling for the dog frantically. Of course, we eventually caught her and proceeded to go to the beach.

I think this was the first realization I had about my mother's behavior. She never changed a routine, even if it caused her chaos.

I WAS NEVER ALONE AMEN

Going to the beach always involved taking Penny's leash off, her running away, and my mother having a meltdown. Why did she just not
take the leash off so the dog could not run away? Doing the same
thing over and over and expecting a different result, I learned later in
life, was called insanity. If you remember from the previous chapter,
this behavior was very dominant in my parents. Rigidity to life's rou-
tines. A bit like the English at war, they always marched in a straight
line, no matter what. They were perfect targets for the enemy, but
they never changed their formation, even when hundreds were being
killed senselessly.

The most exciting thing about living in our new house was all
the kids that played in the street almost every night. I could now have
some friends and be a part of, Whoopi. When I went to school, I did
not cry anymore. However, I was the tallest person in the school. I
would have been around seven years old. My cousin, David, and I
shot up like weeds.

David was the son of Auntie Florence, my father's sister. She
was eight years younger than my dad. I guess when my dad was a
young boy, he was quite a rascal. My grandmother would ask her son,
Ken (my dad), to give Florence her bottle of milk at night. She did
not drink it fast enough for him, so he would drink the milk himself
so he could go off and play. He used to lead a group of young kids
around his neighborhood and scare people who were sitting on their
toilets outside. The kids would climb up on the back wall of people's
gardens and make all kinds of noises. One woman ran into her house
with her knickers down around her feet. We are going back eighty
years. In those days, that was considered naughty.

Let's get back to me. I was told by my mom that I slept a lot
at night. Sometimes, I went to bed by 6.30 p.m. and slept all night
until 7:00 a.m., almost twelve hours of sleep. I used to look forward
to sleeping in on the weekend, especially Sunday morning.

However, on most Sunday mornings as I was snuggled inside
my warm blankets, half asleep and half awake, I heard that voice,
"Anne, Anne are you coming out to play, Anne?" I tried to ignore the
first cry, pulling the blankets over my head. The calling got louder
and sounded more desperate.

It was Peter standing in my backyard, wanting me to come out and play. *It was only 7:00 a.m., for goodness sake, don't you know a girl needs her beauty rest?*

Peter was my best friend. He loved me unconditionally, and when he looked at me with his big brown eyes, he was so happy! We danced together, played outside together; we were inseparable. When it was time to say goodbye for the evening, he never wanted to go. I remember one evening after saying goodbye to Peter, my mother called me in for dinner. Again, my father was never home; we never seemed to eat as a family. Sometimes, my mother would eat early, around 4:00 p.m., or sometimes she would eat with me. After dinner, she would wash the pots and ask me to put them away in the cupboard. The whole event probably took around an hour. I picked up a pile of plates and took them ever so carefully to the cupboard to place them back in their proper spot. As I opened the cupboard, there was Peter. He had been standing for almost an hour in complete silence and had never moved an inch.

"Peter, Peter!" I shouted. "What are you doing in the cupboard?"

He said in a very small voice, "I didn't want to leave you, Anne."

I helped him out of the cupboard and gave him a big hug and reassured him I would see him the next day.

Peter to me was normal in every way. However, he had Down syndrome. He had an amazing capacity to love unconditionally. Unfortunately, he was not "normal enough" to go to a regular school like mine, and was not bad enough to go to a special school for children with this condition. What a dilemma!

Peter had a sister who was quite the tomboy, She even wore boys' underwear. There were about four or five other children that got together and played in the street. I loved the activity, plus I never missed my parents' lack of attention for family life. My father always worked extremely long hours, and my mother always had endless chores to do.

I also befriended a little girl called Casey. She would be about five years old, and I was seven. We used to walk up the street to see Mr. Jenkins who grew prize tomatoes. He would take us into his tomato shed. Maybe that is where I became fascinated watching plants and flowers grow. I thought it was so miraculous how nature worked. Plant a seed, water it, and watch it grow.

We visited Mr. Jenkins regularly until that traumatic event. After seeing the tomatoes in the shed, Casey and I would go into Mr. Jenkins garage. That day, all of a sudden, the biggest, ugliest, most disgusting object came out of Mr. Jenkins pants. My mother had already told me about the "birds and the bees," so I was well aware of what his intention was. He wanted to molest Casey. I took her hand and pulled her away from him. I told him he was a nasty old man and he should be ashamed of himself. Casey had no clue what was going on. Funny thing, we never told our parents.

I also defriended an old lady down the street called Mrs. Graham. She was short in stature, very round, had curly brown hair and wore glasses on the end of her nose. Her response to everything was *see* instead of *yes*. Every time, she looked at you and said, "See," her way of agreeing with what you had just said. Her eyes got as big as the moon and the twinkle in her eye was mesmerizing. I loved visiting her. She had a larger than life personality. I think her family of origin was from Europe. I remember she had the most beautiful backyard. She lived in a bungalow (a house with one story) which was so convenient for older people because they never had to climb stairs to the second floor. I guess I liked spending time with older people. They were the grandparents I never had. Let me rephrase that. I never met my mother's parents and seldom visited by father's.

This is a good time to talk about my grandparents on my father's side. They lived about two hours away in Whitfield, near Manchester. My grandfather was tall and slim, had gray hair, and walked three miles every day. He rarely said a word. My grandmother was about the same height but extremely overweight. I guess they looked like *Laurel and Hardy*.

We visited them every few months. The chain of events that happened during our visit never changed; they were all regimented. As soon as we arrived at their house, Grandad immediately took our dog, Penny, put her on a leash, grasped my hand, and took us both for a walk. But before we set off walking, Grandad loved to rub his unshaved face across mine. His whiskies really hurt, but it made him crack a smile.

He would hold my hand so tight it hurt. I remember shouting out, "Grandad, you're hurting me!"

He said, "I don't want you to run into the road and get run over."

That seemed so ridiculous to me. I was around seven or eight years old; why would I do that? Unfortunately, I passed that behavior down to my children. Even now, with my children (who are young adults), I fear when they cross the street with me that they will not pay attention to the traffic and get run over. It is so amazing how certain behaviors, learned in childhood, never leave you. You can change behaviors with mindful thinking. However, I like being the lioness, very protective of my cubs. If you hurt my cubs, hear me roar!

After the walk, we would go into the house. Immediately, Grandma would open the right door to her side board (wooden cabinet with divisions) and bring out a bag of chocolate for me. Oh boy, what a treat; my mother never let me eat chocolate at home. She said the sugar would rot my teeth out. I think my parents and grandparents talked for a short time, and then it was time for dinner. I remember there were quite a lot of silent moments when nobody knew what to say. You would never know Grandad was my father's dad; there were no loving words. The visit to my grandparents' seemed like a sense of duty from my parent's side.

At this time of my life, I was so happy. I loved my bedroom, my school, and all my friends, especially Peter. However, I was a sickly child. I got chicken pox, whooping cough, and yellow jaundice. So I had to take a lot of time off school. With yellow jaundice, I was in bed for three long boring months. I remember they had to draw my blood all the time. I was poked, prodded, and stuck with needles more than any other time in my life. It seemed like a lifetime lying in my bed. I had no TV in my bedroom, so I have no idea how I passed the time. I do remember the only thing I could eat was clear broth and drink water. Boring!

Peter was really sad he missed his friend. Eventually, when I recovered from the yellow jaundice, I was starving. My mother had caught the flu during this time and had to stay in bed. I would get so hungry and wait impatiently for my dad to come home from work so he could feed me. I remember my mom had cooked a turkey, and my dad fed it to me every night.

When I was around the age of seven, I started ballet lessons. I did not care for it much, too slow and boring. However, we did stage performances. I know because I have a picture of my mom putting hairspray on my hair. The picture was taken by a photographer who worked for the local newspaper. I still have the original clipping from the paper. I think ballet gave me my upright posture. When I walk into a room, I always walk with my shoulders back, and my body reflects a confident person. This serves me well as a speaker. I don't know how long I practiced the art, my mom isn't good at remembering events or time periods. If you try to get her to remember, she gets very frustrated.

The other art I practiced was Elocution Lessons (speech classes) after school, one afternoon a week in a private house. We practiced reading poetry and sections from the Bible. I remember visiting Mrs. Racket, alias Mrs. Frozen, who had an icicle stuck where the sun don't shine. Every painful memory was etched on her face. We would sit in a dark musty smelling corridor, waiting for class to start. There were old paintings of people on the walls and their eyes would follow you wherever you sat. I certainly would not want to be in this house at night. There would probably be screams from children who were disposed of because they did not match up to Mrs. Racket's expectations.

I tried to divert my mind to another thought so fear did not take over and make me run out of her house immediately, dropping my books everywhere, willy-nilly. When it was time for class, her living room door would open ever so quietly, and there she stood. She looked like she was dressed up for Halloween. I know that was just my imagination saying that, but doesn't it sound good? Her dress covered with blood having disposed of the last incompetent student. I told you I had an amazing make-believe world. She said, "Come on in, my pretties." She probably really said, "Come on in, let's get started with class."

I actually loved reciting poems and sections from the Bible. I was a natural. I did not think that at the time. There were about three or four students in the class. We were entered periodically into competitions against other schools. I probably was entered into three or four such events over the course of two years. One competition stands out from all the rest.

I was entered into the Bible reading section of the competition. There were probably eight to ten students competing for the honor certificate (first place). I had to go first, which in all previous competitions, the student speaking first never won. I remember walking up to the stage with my shoulders back and feeling confident. I wish I knew what part of the Bible my speech was about because I was so convicted in the words I spoke. I knew I had done a good job. When I sat down with the other students, they all said, "You will never win, you went first."

I don't remember their unnecessarily cruel remarks bothering me. I listened carefully as each student from competing schools went up to read. Then the three judges compared notes and decided on the students who won the third, second, and first place certificate. They always announced third, second, and then first place. The student with third place went up to the stage, then the student who won second place went up to the stage. Then everyone held their breath.

"The winner of the Bible reading is Anne Hayes!"

I remember being so proud when I walked up to the stage. My internal dialogue went something like this: "Ha! You all thought I couldn't win, because I was first! I showed you!"

I received the certificate from the main judge who complimented me on my success. I really wished at that very moment I had turned and looked at Mrs. Rackets' face. I am sure she must have smiled, even if it was a grimace.

Reading from the Bible during my Elocution lessons must have been the first time I got introduced to God. How did I perceive this awesome God? What did I think about the Bible? I have no recollection if I asked anyone about this new reading material. But I really believed something subconsciously resonated in me. I remember my mother would say prayers over me every night when I was in bed. "God is in, God is out, God is everywhere about. Four angels at each corner of my bed, four angels around my head. God is in, God is out, God is everywhere about." Other than that, she never mentioned the word *God* at any other time.

Yes, life was really grand, living at Hest Bank, Morcambe. I was very happy, except for the fact I grew like a weed. By the age of eight years old, I had a woman's body—thirty-four-inch chest—and by nine years old, I had started my period. Drag! However, I still lived in my make-believe world. I used to dress up in my mother's old clothes and march around the house, pretending to be all grown-up. I guess I had a very expressive personality which I was totally unaware of at the time. I was just being me!

My father at this stage of my life actually came upstairs, when I had gone to bed for the night, and told me jokes. One of my favorites was, "The cat creeped into the cradle, crapped and creeped out."

I would roar with laughter! Then I would say, "Tell me again, Dad."

We both could not stop laughing. He would say after every joke, "Don't tell Mom." She didn't approve of so called "rude words." However, that made no sense, because my father would say out loud in everyday conversation, "I am buggered," if something went wrong. Don't ask me to explain what the b-word means. The meaning is disgusting. Also, my dad would constantly say, "Bloody hell," when irritated by something. I had a very peculiar family.

I probably lived in Morcambe from the age of six to nine. I thought we would live there forever. I never thought there would be any reason to leave. However, one night, when I was in bed getting ready to go to sleep, both my dad and mom came into my bedroom and sat on my bed. They said the unimaginable. "Your dad got a promotion and we have to move."

I said, "I don't want to move. I love my bedroom and all my friends." I guess it was so painful to hear those words, I went into a total blackout for a certain period of time. I never remembered packing my things, I never remembered saying goodbye to Peter. I don't remember leaving the house and driving to our new house in Rochdale. I don't remember walking into my new bedroom and putting my clothes and toys away. What I was feeling, only my subconscious knows; but what transpired later was very disturbing.

CHAPTER 3

Fly, Little Butterfly, Fly

The event that brought me into the present was my mother crying. I remember saying, "What's wrong, Mum?"

"Your grandad has died, and your father has gone to his funeral."

"But why are you crying?" I said, repeating myself. I don't remember my mother's response. My parents, especially my mother, had taught me there is no value in relationships. When I asked if I said goodbye to Peter, my mom said, "I don't know." That response really devastated me. Again, another seed was planted. My feelings didn't count.

I would now be around nine years old and I started having nightmares. The first sensation I felt was my skin feeling tight and irritated all over my body; then this disgusting taste came into my mouth, and then, finally, the huge boulders would come rolling over my whole body, trying to suffocate me. My chest got tight, I was full of fear, and at that point, when I felt I was taking my last breath of air, I would wake up in a cold sweat. My heart was beating rapidly. I was gasping for air. These nightmares lasted for years. I imagine they were associated with the move from Morcambe to Rochdale.

We had always lived in beautiful clean areas; however, Rochdale was quite dark, gloomy, and somewhat dirty. It rained all the time. Rochdale is a town on the outskirts of Manchester, which is an industrial city. We lived in a bungalow which I didn't like. I was used to walking upstairs to bed. There were no children that played in the street. There was one family that my mother befriended, and they had four girls. However, we never played together, which I thought was odd.

I attended a public school. The school building was about ten to fourteen stories high. I hated walking up the stairs because the steps were open, and as you walked up, you could see all the way down. I hated heights. I looked so peculiar when trying to walk down the stairs. I would sit down on my bottom and scoot myself from one step to another. It took forever as I watched all the students almost fly down the stairs.

However, this school was a really cool school. They had music playing in one of the downstairs rooms. They had flashing lights and people were dancing to their hearts content on their lunch breaks. Amazing, right? There was also a group of us who walked to the local park and played kiss-catch. There was one peculiar boy who I thought was so fine. All the girls would have to put their hands on the large oak tree that stood in the middle of the park. Then on the count of five, we had to run like hell, hoping none of the boys would catch us and kiss us. That was daring in those days. Of course, secretly, we all wanted to be caught.

I would purposely run in the direction of Devin, my body full of electricity and utter excitement at the thought of being caught. When I saw he was running toward me, I would slow down a little, not too much; I wasn't going to make it that easy. If he was going to kiss me, the chase had to be somewhat challenging. I wasn't one of those "loose girls" I want you to know. When I could not run any more, Devin bolted in the air and landed straight on top of me. Funny thing, he had a hard time giving me a kiss. It was a very awkward moment for both of us.

So even though I did not like Rochdale, my new school made up for it. It was very different. There were hundreds of children at that school. I remember a couple of kids calling me Pinocchio. They thought I had a long nose. Idiots! There used to be fights in the schoolyard, and hundreds of kids would come and circle the two students fighting. It was scary! I had never seen anything like that before.

I remember attending drama class. We would have to practice skits. I got partnered off with a really tall boy. When I stood next to him, my face came up to his chest. The theme of the skit was the boy had been unfaithful to the girl, and we were supposed to act it out impromptu. I had thought over and over how could I make our performance unique. Then I got the idea! Now all I had to do was wait for the day to perform. When the day came, I walked on stage, I was composed; then the act began. I remember sitting on a bench and having to listen to my partner confess he had gone out with another girl and that he was very sorry. I had replied, "How do I know your sorry?"

He replied, "But I am."

I said, "I don't think you are." And I slowly pulled out a toy gun. I said "Get on your knees," pointing the gun at his head.

Luckily for me, my acting partner got on his knees and went along with the surprise. I wish you could have been there, I put on quite a show! In the end, I shot him several times. He was amazing, staggering across stage, like they do in the movies, until he dropped dead! The sound crew went ballistic! The noise of the toy gun going off really messed with their delicate sound equipment. I guess I was somewhat of a rebel at heart. I hated how my mother always wanted me to be the "good little girl who doesn't cause any problems." Yuck!

I would go on a school bus to my public school. In fact, there were two buses that stopped at the end of my street to pick up students. The same two buses would pick up students at the school at the end of the day and take them back home. Well, there was a student at the school called Daniel Fisher, the school bully. I tried to avoid jumping onto the same bus as him on the way home. He lived a few houses away from me, so we both got off at the same bus stop. When that unfortunate encounter happened, he would thump me in the stomach a couple of times and then ran home. This went on for a few weeks, so I devised a plan.

I jumped onto the first school bus that was taking students home. After I got off, I hid in the bushes. I waited for Daniel Fisher to get off the second school bus. I had to get my timing perfect to fulfill my plan. He jumped off the bus and started walking home, and as he turned the corner, *wham!* I swung my school bag straight for his head. He stopped abruptly, then suddenly one lens fell out of his glasses, and then the other lens fell to the ground. He was in total shock! He picked the lenses up and ran home. Mission accomplished! He never bothered me again. Let people underestimate you so you can make a move when people least expect it.

Then, when I was around ten years old, one single decision was made and my life changed forever. My mother came up with the bright idea that I needed to get a good education and that my current school was simply not going to measure up.

My parents told me they were going to send me to Rishworth School, a private school, in Yorkshire. It was a boarding school, but I was going to be a day student. Students attended there from all over the world. There was a coach that left from downtown Rochdale every day to the school. It would take an hour to get there and an hour back. Worst of all, there was school Saturday morning—what a deplorable thing.

The first day I arrived at the school, my heart sunk. The school was a giant red-stoned building. It was probably a hundred years old. It spread out over quite a large acreage. There was the main building where everyone gathered in the morning to say prayers. Once again, God was introduced into my life. There were a few classrooms in that building. The cafeteria was on the lower level. The rest of the classrooms were scattered all around, some in red-stoned buildings, some were portable mobiles. The dorms where students lived were in separate buildings. The most disturbing thing was when I entered my first classroom. All the girls sat on one side of the room, and all the boys were on the other. What was this all about? I hated this idea.

I had to study hard every night for three long hours. The material was so much harder than the work I had done at my previous school. School days were very long. I left the house around 7:00 a.m. and returned around 6:00 p.m. Then it was dinner, study, bath, and bed. I became more and more despondent. Sometimes when I came home from school, I wanted to talk to my mom. She would just yell at me, "You have got your health, what more do you want? Go to your room!" That was standard procedure. "Don't be happy, don't be sad, don't complain, don't interrupt me." Life had gotten very lonely for me. All work and no play made Anne a very unhappy girl.

I had no friends in the neighborhood. I would wait at the window every night, waiting for my dad to come home from work. *Maybe today he will pay attention to me.* Nope, he could not wait to get to his television. No one was allowed to talk during dinner or the rest of the night. He wanted complete silence, and if someone talked, they were yelled at.

My father watched me when I ate, and if I hit my teeth with my fork, I got slapped. I had to walk around the house on egg shells. I lived in fear. I thought if I made too much noise, I would have to leave home. I had to have a shower by a certain time. I was a prisoner, and there did not seem any way to get out.

At night, when I went to bed, I would cry myself to sleep. Sometimes I pretended my bed was a boat, and I travelled to different islands to visit friends. Summer vacations were the worst. Three months off school and nothing to do. I did, however, have my dog, Penny, to play with which occupied some of the time.

Sometimes, I would ask my mother to make lunch for us and pretend we were having a picnic. I was desperate for some company. After we had eaten, she would always say, "That was a waste of time. I could have been doing something better."

I felt so unlovable. No brothers or sisters, no friends, and even my own mother did not want to talk to me. To make matters worse, one afternoon when I was sitting in the kitchen, eating my lunch, she said, "You know the best years of my life were before you were born."

I wanted to disappear into the ground and never return. I asked myself, "Why was I born?"

I developed an eating disorder in my teenage years. I would eat for comfort and I put on quite a lot of weight. My father would sit in his chair and call me fatso.

My father used to love to torment me. One night, we watched Dracula, and I was so frightened. I pretended the movie did not bother me, and when it ended, I got up and went to bed expressionless. Once I got into my bedroom, I gave a sigh of relief. Suddenly, there was a knock at my door. I opened the door and on the floor was a black dress being pulled along the ground. I screamed and ran into the bathroom. A bucket had been placed on top of the door, so when I opened it, it fell on my head. I screamed really loud this time and ran back into my bedroom. My father was roaring with laughter.

I decided it was time to run away from home. I carefully planned out all the things I was going to take with me. I stood at my bedroom window, crying and feeling all alone. Then very quietly, I heard a tiny voice. It said "Don't run away. You have nowhere to go and no money. When you are older, you will go off to a far-off land and be happy."

I stood very still. I asked myself, "Did I really hear that? Or was that my imagination?" Well, the voice definitely got my attention. I forgot all about running away. I got into bed and went to sleep.

The time period from the age of ten to seventeen was very dark, sad, and lonely. I felt hopeless and helpless and had no one to turn to. I hated my life. My father's job was too stressful for him. He just could not deal with the pressure. So everyone suffered his rage and restlessness.

Many times in my early teenage years, I would stand at my bedroom window and hear the voice saying, "Don't worry, you will be going off to a faraway land and you will have a happy life."

I thought to myself, *My family doesn't know anyone in a faraway land*. The voice was not audible, but I understood complete sentences.

In the English education, students studied for O levels in various subjects, and at the age of sixteen had to take a written test to take further education. Because my birthday falls on November, I started school a year early. So at the age of fifteen, I took the tests and passed ten O levels which was unheard of. The average student got seven.

Around sixteen years old, I became a prefect at my school. A prefect was someone assigned to look over and monitor younger students entering the school. All prefects had an extra snack time around 4:00 p.m. Yummy! Lots of sugary comfort foods to help with my eating disorder. I definitely was not comfortable in my own skin and had low self-esteem. I always tried to skip the exercise classes or PE classes (English equivalent).

It was a very strict school. I remember in English class, a student had done something wrong, so the English teacher took his head and slammed it into his desk. Of course, that was over forty years ago.

I remember there was the occasional "Disco night" at the school. For one dance, my mother bought me my first set of jeans. It was embroidered on the pockets. I remember walking into the place thinking I was the cat's meow. Some of the students noticed me dancing and commented on my outfit and my dance moves. Let me tell you, I really know how to shake my booty!

I studied the next two years for my A levels but only passed Chemistry. I really stopped studying. I was so burnt out from my O levels. Later, I did study for my biology class and passed it. I never got the grades to go to university. Thank goodness. I would have never survived.

I was the most depressed I had ever been. I wore big clothes to cover my large body. I hardly spoke to my parents, and if they ever asked me anything, I would snap back at them. I had really grown to resent them, especially my mother. Why my parents had me was very difficult to understand. They did not enjoy my company, I spent most of my time in my bedroom, and I could do nothing right.

I took a secretarial course and ended up working for three doctors at a local hospital. I decided to move out of my parents' house at around twenty-one years old when I answered an ad in the local newspaper that said "Roommate Needed." The arrangement did not last long. I found her in the bath with another woman. I moved into another roommate situation, and that did not work out either. Eventually, I got my own apartment. It was within walking distance of Rochdale Infirmary where I worked.

I decided to lose my excess weight, dye my hair blonde, and change my clothing choices. Wow, what a difference! People would actually look at me as I was walking by.

I had a part-time job working in a local bar. It was a few minutes' walk up the street from my apartment. I worked behind the bar, serving drinks. I dated the owner's son; he was delicious!

It was depressing living in my part of the country. It rained all the time and we had about six weeks of sunshine in the summer. People would go to work, go to the bar after work, get drunk, go home to bed, and start the routine all over again the next day. What a waste of a life.

My mother would unexpectedly show up at my apartment unannounced, which really bothered me. My parents never treated me with respect. They always treated me like I was ten years old. She would bring me clean sheets for my bed, but it was her excuse to snoop around. One day, she found an empty condom package, and that was it; she vowed never to speak to me again. However, after some time, she forgave me. Hallelujah!

By this time, I could not even stand to be around my parents. My mother had totally destroyed my self-worth. "You have the wrong boyfriend, you wear the wrong clothes, you wear the wrong makeup." She went on and on.

My father always called me stupid. He could no longer call me fatso since I had lost my excess fat. They both used me as a punching bag. If my father paid attention to me, my mother was jealous; if my mother paid attention to me, my father was jealous.

They had to control everything. They were also very fearful people (maybe because of World War II). Every window in the house was locked down with a separate key. There were two doors you had to go through to get into the back of the house; and two doors to go through to get into the front of the house. Every electrical device had to be unplugged when we left the house or else the whole house was going to burn down while we were gone. This ritual was very frightening to me when I was a young child. I didn't know if I would still have a bedroom when we came back from the store. Every night, a burglar alarm was set. It was like Fort Knox.

It was not apparent to me at this time that my parents must have gone through some trauma to have such bizarre behaviors. All I knew was when I was around them, I was a complete mess and looked like I was on the verge of a nervous breakdown. I simply could not go on this way.

I decided I needed to leave the country. I had an idea of becoming an au pair and working overseas. I wanted to go to America but I could not find a company that arranged for au pairs to go over there. I had decided to go to Germany.

Unbeknownst to me, my mother had run into a lady whose friend was working as an au pair in Florida. I guess my mother was very reluctant to inform me of this connection. However, when it became apparent I was not going to be swayed to stay in England, she informed me of the possible contact in America. The au pair in Florida found me a job, and I got ready to leave my homeland.

I really felt like I had no choice. I was very fearful of going to a different country all by myself. I had never gone anywhere alone. But the pain I would experience facing the unknown was far less than staying in an insane asylum with my parents.

I remember the cramps in my stomach and my head spinning with anxiety as I packed my bags to leave. As I walked out of the backdoor of my parents' house, my mother said, "You are not welcome back here. You make your bed. You lie in it."

My father said, "You can't leave. You need to stay here and look after me. I will have to look for another daughter."

Well, that was the end of that!

CHAPTER 4

Step Carefully Around Strangers

A taxi driver took me to the airport. I checked in at the airline counter. As my bags disappeared down the conveyor belt, my heart sunk into my stomach.

Reality set in; there was no turning back now. I simply had to put one foot in front of another. I waited at the appropriate gate number to board my plane. "Boarding all passengers on Flight 507 to Florida," the airline stewardess announced.

I remember very clearly as I walked through the gate to the aircraft saying to myself, "I will never come back here to live again."

The plane ride to Florida was excruciatingly painful. I threw up all the way there; fear had really set in. What was I doing? What would the family be like that was waiting for me at the airport? My mind was racing with all these negative thoughts. The plane ride seemed to last forever.

The plane finally landed. Walking from the plane through the disembarking corridor to the gate where the family was waiting for me was like walking to my execution. There they were: a family with three children, and they were not of American descent. I tried to hold back the tears. I wanted to run away! I thought I had made the biggest mistake of my life coming to the United States. I knew immediately I was not going to get along with the mother. She looked uptight and unhappy.

We arrived at their house. It was a very large house with a swimming pool in the backyard. I was escorted to my room. I closed the bedroom door and threw myself on the bed, crying profusely.

When it was dinner time, I came into the kitchen to eat. The mother wanted me to eat in a separate room (so unfriendly), but the kids insisted I join them at the family table.

I was very homesick, but what was I going to do? The mother worked me six days a week, fourteen hours a day. I didn't know I was going to be treated like a slave.

When I eventually met the woman who got me the job and told her the conditions I was working under, she seemed surprised. She then informed me the family had twelve different au pairs over the last twelve months. I was angry and said, "Why would you put me in such a bad situation?"

She said, "I thought it was the au pairs that were at fault, not the mother!"

What a complete, diabolical, idiotic, uncalled situation I was in!

I arrived in Florida in October 1983. I worked hard cleaning the house, doing the laundry, babysitting for very little pay. I rarely got to go out and have any fun. The mother worked me Christmas Day because their religion did not celebrate that holiday. The reputation of that religion was confirmed in concrete. Never once when I lived in England did I think I was sending correspondence to a non-American family. Remember, I could not return home. I would not be welcomed. It became apparent later that it was a good thing.

I have no idea whatsoever how a friend of a friend in England found out where I was working. Her name was Brittany. I had not told anyone in England the address I was going to. That was a miracle; or was it something greater than myself in control of my destiny?

Brittany called me up and we went out for a drink. She was definitely a breath of fresh air, someone English; thank goodness! We really partied every chance we could. We would always go to happy hour at the various local bars. Liquor was only a quarter a shot, and we knew how to drink. Remember, English people are used to drinking in pubs a lot!

However, one day, I had drunk way too much and got into my car. I was driving along, feeling really happy. Unfortunately, from a lapse of memory, I thought I was in England, and when I saw three cars in three different lanes driving toward me, I frantically realized I was driving on the wrong side of the road. I wasn't in England anymore! I had the awful realization I was not going to be able to get out of this one. Then miraculously, in a split-second, I was driving on the other side of the road in the right direction. Wow, how did that happen? I thanked my lucky stars.

Another undeniable, unexplainable, unbelievable event that happened, which could have changed the course of my life forever, was one evening when I was driving home intoxicated. Just thinking about this incident, which happened thirty years ago, makes my whole body shake and my heart race with terror.

It was one evening when Brittany and I went to happy hour at a pub. Usually, one would be a designated driver, but this time we both drank to excess. After we parted ways, we both got into our own vehicles and drove home. I was so drunk I ran off the road a couple of times. Then suddenly, there were flashing lights behind me and the police pulled me over. I have no idea what words were exchanged.

Florida police are very strict; loss of license and deportation could have been in store for me. Instead, they let me go, and I drove home. Now if you are an agnostic or atheist reading this book, you cannot say that was luck. A serious question must be entering your head. How can that happen?

I came into America on a six-month visitor's visa. I did not have a work visa; that is why some families took advantage of au pairs. If you did not comply to the rules, they would turn you into Immigration. Big mistake on my part working for a family with no contract. They could set their own unreasonable job requirements.

One day, the family said they were taking a few days' vacation to Naples, a town on the other side of Florida, and asked if I would like to come along. They were going to celebrate New Years'. I said yes; I had nothing else to do. What I did not know was on New Year's Eve, I would have to take twelve children to dinner. Three other families had joined them, and I was given the job of looking after them all.

36

I was offered no extra money from my family or the other families. I unfortunately had developed a real distaste for this particular race of people.

Needless to say, the dinner was chaotic. The age of the children ranged from two to fourteen years old. It was definitely a challenge just keeping them seated at the table.

After dinner, we all had to pile into one bedroom. Fun, fun, fun! Unfortunately, two of the teenagers snuck out of the bedroom when I wasn't looking. The youngest child of the family I was enslaved to was in bed. I told her older brother to sit next to the bed and watch her until I came back with the defiant teenagers. I left the bedroom and went downstairs looking for the two girls. As I went around the corner to the main lobby, who did I bump into? Yes, the family I was working for.

Unfortunately, as soon as I left the bedroom, the two-year-old had awakened and was crying. The family told me, "Our children come first. You did not need to go looking for the teenagers." I was damned if I did and damned if I didn't. I was fired!

When we got home, they gave me a couple of days to pack and leave. I called Brittany and told her the situation. She said, "Why don't you go to California? I can get you a job over there."

"What?"

"Yes, you will love it over there."

I told her to make some enquiries. I didn't have anything to lose. However, where was I going to live in the meantime?

During my visit to a local bar, I had met a girl who was working in a restaurant which was family-owned. I felt compelled to call her and tell her my situation. She said, "I will ask the family I work for if you can stay with them until you hear from a family in California."

That did not seem feasible. Who was going to let a stranger stay in their house for free? Again, I reminded myself I didn't have any alternative choices. I could not go home and I had no money to stay in a hotel.

I thanked my lucky stars—the family said yes. So I packed my bags and left the house where I had been working and went to live with the Parkinson family. The family was so kind to me. They said

I could live with them as long as I needed to until I got my life in order. They were definitely heaven-sent.

Within five days, a family contacted me from California and offered me a job. I feared that I did not have enough money for the airfare. I contacted the local airport and found out they were running a discounted airfare to California for $200. All the money I had in my pocket was $230, and the new family were only offering me a job for $60 a week. Talk about balancing on a tight rope with no safety net! I bought the ticket and off I went to California.

Again my body was full of fear. I asked myself, "Am I going to be safe not really knowing the family I am going to work for?" What was I getting myself into again?

The family greeted me at the airport. Thank goodness they were American. The family consisted of two parents and three children. They seemed nice, and after welcoming me, we drove to their house. As we were travelling in the car, I was awestruck with California. The scenery was breathtaking! I loved the mountains and the lush landscape. I said to myself, "I can live here."

When we got to their house, they informed me of all the duties they wanted me to fulfill during my stay. They had never had an au pair before. They hired me because the parents wanted to go on a three-week vacation to Europe and leave the children with me. Unfortunately, the mother did not work. What was most disturbing was she had absolutely no control over her children. She never set boundaries with them, disciplined them, and they literally had the run of the house. Oh boy, this was going to be extremely challenging. Two different women giving them instructions? They most definitely rebelled against that. They had trained their mother well. The children were in charge, and in their minds, nothing was going to change.

Help! There was no way I was going to be left alone with these out of control kids. I could see they were a disaster waiting to happen and I certainly did not want to be put in such a precarious situation.

I started looking around for a different job, which was extremely hard to do, because all eyes were watching me. I called numerous places and went on one interview. The job entailed looking after the family when the mother, who was an airline stewardess, went away for four days at a time. I unfortunately did not get the job. I struggled away at my present job but became increasingly frustrated at the lack of structure around everyday life. I actually felt sorry for the mother who would simply collapse at the end of each day from complete exhaustion.

During the next few days, I had this nagging feeling that I should call the family back. The airline stewardess chose another girl for the job. I kept trying to dismiss the thought when it came up but eventually picked up the phone in an attempt to stop my monkey mind. The mother, Paulina, answered the phone and said, "Thank goodness you called back. We want you for the job." The girl they wanted to hire took another job.

This job came up in the nick of time. The family I was working for had become very suspicious of the unexplained phone numbers on their phone bill. I was waiting for them to approach me and ask me to explain why I had called all these different numbers. I thought I was calling local numbers that were free of charge.

I sat down with the parents and explained in detail to them why I simply could not be left in charge of their children while they were on vacation. I said I would give them a two-week notice so they could find someone else to hire. The father was very understanding. The mother, on the other hand, told me to pack my bags immediately and leave.

I remember putting my suitcases on my bed and packing my clothes as if it happened yesterday. By this time, I had become used to unstable living accommodations and was quite composed while the mother continued cursing me out.

I left the house quietly and drove to my next job. I was now living in Lafayette, California. It was such a beautiful place to live. There were walking trails and enchanting boutique shops. Wild flowers grew everywhere, and the sun was always shining. I said to myself, "I'm not in England anymore. I am in paradise."

I made the mistake once again of working for a family who had never hired an au pair before. A word of advice: don't put yourself in a position where you become the guinea pig. The family had an eighteen-month-old baby girl. Her name was Casey. She definitely did not like me. She had never had anyone take care of her other than her parents. Her mother, Paulina, was extremely protective of her baby girl. After one week, the family announced they wanted me to leave. I said no indignantly. "You haven't given me a chance." It was very stressful when the parents went to work and Casey cried and held onto their clothes for dear life.

So when they went to work that day, it called for drastic measures. I needed this job and I wasn't about to leave. I took Casey and placed her on the counter. I told her, "I am the boss, and you will do as I say." I further told her, "If you cause me any problems whatsoever, I will throw you across the room onto the couch." Of course, I would never do that, but she didn't know that.

The next morning at breakfast, when her parents were about to leave for work, Casey shouted "Bye-bye, stay with Anne." We were all shocked, especially me. Casey and I became best of friends. She followed me everywhere. I am actually extremely good with children, because I still have that childlike spirit.

Another eighteen-month-old little girl named Tory soon joined us. Looking after Tory as well as Casey allowed me to make extra money. I have to tell you, looking after those two little girls was so much fun. We danced, sang, painted pictures, and did puzzles. I read to them a lot. I loved seeing their sweet angelic faces looking at me as I read.

When I babysat Tory, she would walk through the front door and say, "Anne, oh, Anne" with the sweetest smile. I don't think anybody else's morning welcome has warmed my heart like Tory's did. I was her whole world. Those were very special days.

I got to finally relax. Casey's parents thought I was the bees knees. They told me I was the best thing that had ever happened to them. *Sure, you wanted to kick me out two weeks ago.*

Because Paulina only worked four days straight, twice a month, I had a lot of time off. I would go to the local bars to meet people. I started dating all kinds of different guys. However, I never slept with any of them. I told them they had to date other girls for that. Why? Because they were just allowing life to take them wherever. I intuitively knew people with no direction were not reliable and I should not invest any emotional energy into them.

However, I think Stewart is worth a mention. He rode a Harley-Davidson motorcycle, and literally, one day, he said "Do you want to go for a ride?"

I had never ridden on the back of a bike before, so I said yes. I hopped on the back and he literally rode to Lake Tahoe. I was shocked. All the maneuvers he did on that bike—me having no experience—caused me to just shut my eyes and hold on for dear life. It was definitely worth the ride! Lake Tahoe was breathtaking!

A couple of months later, the family announced there was going to be a giant company picnic at Lake Berryessa. All the local air-conditioning companies and equipment distributors were getting together. They were going and wanted me to accompany them so they could introduce me to Mark. I was not too thrilled with the idea, but you know what they say: a change is as good as a rest.

The day of the picnic was glorious. The sun was shining and the temperature was perfect. There were lots of people at the event. I was not very comfortable in my own skin, because I did not know anyone. I sat down on the grass with Mr. and Mrs. Kensington (Paulina and her husband) and Casey. It was very beautiful sitting next to the lake.

Around an hour later, it was lunchtime. There was tons of food. I remember getting a plate of barbecued chicken, beans, and potato salad. I sat down by myself to eat. I was so hungry I could have eaten a cow. I ate like I had not been fed for a week. Yum! The food was delicious! However, I noticed some guys playing football, and their ball was getting really close to my head. So I got up and went to sit near a tree. That was better; no one to disturb me. Now where was I? Oh yes, eating the fatted calf!

A few minutes later, a man came over to talk to me. He was the one kicking the ball near my head. I cannot recall the conversation we had. About half an hour later, my family came over and told me it was time to go. I gathered my things together and got ready to leave with them. They pointed out the man I was talking to was Mark, the guy they wanted to introduce me to. I was not impressed.

Before I was able to walk over to the car with Mr. and Mrs. Kensington, Paulina looked straight at Mark and said, "I am sure someone else could take you home."

"Yes," said Mark, "I can drive her home."

I was definitely not happy. I told Paulina, "I don't even know him. I don't think it is a good idea."

She reassured me everything would be okay.

I left the picnic, in protest, with Mark. We were going to drive back to his apartment in Fairfield and then go out for the evening. He drove home really fast. I think he was trying to impress me. The impression I formed was, *What an idiot.* Every time he drove around a corner, he ended up on the other side of the road. I thought, *If there is a God, please help me stay alive.*

When we got back to his messy apartment, his man cave, we got changed and went out. Mark liked to talk a lot. He had great plans for his life. He was going to build a house. He was going to study and get certificates that would allow him to advance in the heating and air-conditioning business. He was very different from other guys I had dated. He had drive and ambition; now that impressed me. It was as if he was saying, "I want to do all this but with someone." He was twenty-nine years old, and I was twenty-four at the time. Later, he drove me home and we said we would stay in contact.

A few days later, Mark phoned me, and we arranged to meet the next weekend. He was interesting to talk to. His mind never stopped thinking. He asked me, "What plans do you have?"

My six-month visitor's visa was about to expire, so I said jokingly, "I need someone to marry me so I can stay in the country."

Mark announced, "I will marry you!"

I said, "Okay." I always had to make decisions to survive; not healthy decisions. I always felt I had no choices. No money, no place to go—a bad situation to be in.

During the next week, Mark started having second thoughts. He thought to himself, *What am I doing?* So one day, while he was sitting in his car, something unexplainable happened. This is how Mark described the incident to me.

"I was sitting in my car, and suddenly, I was paralyzed. I could not move my arms and legs. I could not turn my head. Then I was given a vision of my life with you and knew everything would work out fine." This had never happened to him before. The story of my life should be becoming more and more curious to anyone reading this book.

So we planned to go to Reno the next weekend, August 4, 1984, and get married. We met on the Fourth of July and were getting married one month later. This was the start of a new chapter in my life.

CHAPTER 5

Wherever You Are, There You Will Be

So the next weekend, I packed my bags for an overnight stay in Reno. I didn't buy a new dress, I just wore one I had.

I drove over to Fairfield to meet Mark. When he came out of his apartment, he looked like a wild man. He wore tight jeans, no shirt with an open denim vest, and his hair was like an afro. What a sight to behold; and that was my future husband! *If there is a God, please help me.*

Actually, the ride up to Reno was great fun. Mark sang to me all the way there. The singing put us both at ease.

We booked into a hotel and got dressed for the big day. We went to a local chapel in the area to get married. Mark appeared very sincere and emotional when he said his vows. For me, it was just a matter of necessity so I could stay in the country. If Mark had not come into my life, I don't know what I would have done.

After the ceremony, we signed all the papers but needed a witness and wondered what we could do. It was a complete and refreshing surprise when Mr. and Mrs. Kensington showed up to be our witnesses. Wow, they drove all the way here to support us and with a picnic basket full of food and wine to boot!

We all sat out on the lawn in front of the chapel. We laughed and really enjoyed the time together. If they had not shown up, we probably would not have had any wedding pictures for keepsakes.

We went to see Gladys Knight in concert on our wedding night. The concert was amazing! I can't remember how long we stayed in Reno, just that the wine was flowing and plentiful.

Eventually, it was time to go home. I drove back to Lafayette to pack all my things, and Mark agreed to pick me up a few days later. Obviously, the family would need to find someone else to work for them. I was not sad to leave. I was happy to no longer be an au pair. Too much work and too little pay. They found an Irish girl to take over the position.

The evening arrived when Mark was to pick me up. He was so late, I feared he was not going to show up. He eventually arrived with flowers in hand. That made me feel special.

I said goodbye to the family and off I went into the unknown once again. I didn't know who Mark really was. He did not come with a portfolio. We lived in low income apartments off East Tabor in Fairfield.

Mark introduced me to all his pot-smoking friends. Of course, I had started participating in this recreational activity. Sometimes, when they really started partying, cocaine came on the scene. What a great influence my new husband was! Having had a somewhat sheltered life, this was most definitely mind-blowing, literally!

Mark worked for a local heating and air-conditioning company as a technician doing service calls. He was an extremely hard worker. He asked me if he was capable of running his own company. I said, "Sure you are. You can do it." So he started studying for his contractor's license. It was really hard for him working full-time and going to college at night. Sometimes, he could hardly make it to bed. He was so exhausted.

Before he left his present job, we qualified to buy a house and we took full advantage of that or else it could be years before we would qualify again. We moved to Vacaville and bought a three-bedroom tract home; to me, it was heaven—a place of our own, what a blessing! The house backed up to a hill which made it even better; no neighbors peering in.

Mark got his contractor's license and started his own business. He was very conscientious and worked extremely diligently to get new customers and reap some profit.

I applied to Macy's to get a job, but they turned me down. I was very despondent about the rejection. However, Mark said, "Go back and apply again. Don't take no for an answer." If there was one thing that he taught me, it was no doesn't mean no. So I went back to Macy's and they hired me to work in the cosmetics department selling Biotherm skin products. It was fun and I loved the products. I am a good salesperson, if you hadn't already guessed.

Life was good; however, I always had negative thinking going on. In some ways, I was capable of fulfilling a task but personally I never felt a part of it. Another major issue that affected our marriage was no matter how many times Mark said he loved me, I did not hear it. If my parents did not love me, then no one was going to love me. I had the core belief that I was not *lovable*.

From age twenty-five to twenty-nine, I actually would plan how I could depart from this world. I appeared happy at times but was very depressed when I was alone. I would do anything to try and prevent feeling like "little Anne" who had been sent to her room and was crying from loneliness.

One day, Mark got the great idea of buying a dog. He went to a private breeder who was selling Golden Retrievers. He picked out one of the pups. He was not able to bring the puppy home right away. I think because it had not had all his required inoculation shots. However, when Mark went back to bring the puppy home, the owner tried to switch the puppies. Too bad, it was really hard to get one over on Mark, and he stood his ground insisting this was not the dog he had picked out. The owner eventually gave him the right puppy.

When Mark came home with that bundle of joy, I was in love! No, *really* in love. We called him Charlie, and he fit in my lap perfectly. Charlie became my constant companion. We were inseparable. He was just what the doctor ordered to cure my loneliness. Charlie grew and grew and grew to over a hundred pounds. Unfortunately, he always thought of himself as a puppy and would back up slowly and sit on my lap. He was so heavy. He was so mild-mannered, but when Mark pretended to attack me, he would become vicious-looking, showing all his teeth and growling. He got ready to defend me at all costs.

For some unexplainable reason, other dogs liked to attack Charlie. I did not realize it until this moment, but this had happened to me in my life. Some unhappy people take an instant dislike to me for no reason. With Charlie, other dogs had no chance of winning a fight. He would simply stand on top of them and hold his teeth close to their throat but not press down. I never thought some dogs were envious of other dogs, but they are.

I do want to tell you about one incident that happened when we lived in Vacaville. I would take Charlie for a walk every day. We would pass by this particular house, and the Golden Retriever would viciously bark at us. It was left in the backyard almost all the time when it's owners went to work. One day, the dog got out and ran to our front yard where Charlie was playing. This was a very scary dog fight. My parents were visiting at the time from England. The two dogs were locked together with their teeth, so my mother decided to get hold of the other dog's tail in an attempt to break them apart. It did not work, so I got the hosepipe and sprayed them with water; that did not work.

The dog fight had been going on for quite a while now, and everyone was in a state of fear. So I did what I usually do when drastic measures need to be taken. I went into the garage, found the largest shovel I could, and slammed it on top of the other dog's head. It broke up the fight and the other dog ran home. Charlie had no scratches on him, thank goodness.

However, the owner of the other dog had to take his dog to the animal hospital. This time, Charlie had sunk his teeth into the dog's neck; he had no choice if he wanted to survive.

This reminds me that we always need to be awake, because the enemy is always waiting to attack when we least expect it. I never wanted to live my life like that, being on guard, but it had proven to be necessary to stay emotionally balanced. One thing I do daily is visualize a healing protective white light around me.

So you are probably wondering how my parents came onto the scene. When Mark and I got married, we did not tell anyone for six months. We wanted to get some sure footing. When my parents were told, my father was extremely angry. However, I was their only child, so they wanted to stay in contact and, of course, came out to visit me. They actually came to visit almost every year for fifteen years. In the beginning, I could hardly stand being in their presence. I had built up so much anger toward them. This is a severe problem within families today, the lack of communication. One party looks at a situation one way and the other another way.

They thought they were great parents. I thought they were cold, non-empathetic, and had no love in their hearts for anyone, especially me. Unless both parties can have the courage to talk about problems, the white giant elephant sits in the living room and never leaves.

After working at Macy's a few months, I met the area manager who worked directly for Biotherm. She was fabulous, and we got along famously. She offered me a freelance position of travelling to various Macy's stores in the Bay area to sell Biotherm. I loved the position! I worked four days a week, five hours a day.

At around the age of twenty-five, my boss from Biotherm, Stacy, and her husband invited Mark and myself to go on a trip with them to Mexico. Now they were millionaires, so this was going to be a trip of a lifetime. The trip involved literally getting on a three-mast galleon ship and sailing around the Mexican coastline.

We met them in La Paz, Mexico, at the airport. They promptly took us to the boat. There were six of us taking the trip. The boat was amazing! It had giant white sails, so the wind was the only source of power. They had a very experienced captain on board, a cook, and four or five extra helpers. The decks were solid mahogany wood, and they gleamed from hours of polishing. All the rigging was methodically taken out and put back in its precise place. There were sun beds for tanning, tables, and chairs for dining or playing cards. There was a giant barbecue stove where meat, chicken, or their daily catch was cooked. The fresh fish dinners were delicious.

Below the deck were the State rooms where people slept. Mark and I were given a beautiful room to stay in. At night, the boat would rock us to sleep. I had never suffered from motion sickness, so I had no problems dealing with the motion of the ocean.

We set sail almost immediately, and I left all my worries at the dock. Mark struggled with having no control with the daily itinerary. As for me, not having to think was a vacation all to itself.

We travelled to various ports along the coast. To get from the ship to land, we would hop onto a motor boat attached to the back of the ship. It was like travelling with the rich and famous.

I was literally in paradise, eating at various restaurants in the different ports. I loved travelling around Mexico—seeing all the different brightly colored buildings, the old weathered faces of the local fishermen who would be coming back to shore with their daily catch, the locals lining up on the dock to buy their fish for the day, the women who wore a multitude of scarves displaying all the colors of the rainbow, the noise coming from the local taverns where the men drank and laughed about the tales of old, the incredible ambiance of the Mexican way of life.

On this trip, I had an experience of a lifetime. The ship stopped at a small island where sea lions lived. They were swimming all around the ship. The crew got us suited up with wet suits, snorkel equipment, and fins. We were all going to get into the water. Now I cannot swim, but put fins on me, and I can swim like a mermaid. Once I got into the water, I started snorkeling, and the ocean turned into a magical playground. I was swimming with the sea lions; there was one below me, one on either side of me, and there appeared to be hundreds around me. I was moving through the water like I was a seasoned swimmer. I was watching them swim with me. Their bodies were huge and they loved our comradeship. I was swimming so quickly, I lost track of time and moved away from the group.

Eventually, one of the crew members got my attention and called me back to the ship. They were not happy that I moved away from the group. They said where there were sea lions, there were sharks. Oh, boy, glad they didn't tell me that before I got into the water.

I love the ocean, especially sailing on it. I also go hiking along the northern Californian coastline several times a year. The ocean inspires awareness of self and how I play an important part in the whole of humanity. It activates my imagination. If you can dream it, you can manifest it.

During my late twenties, I was trying to acclimate to living in California. It was very different from living in England. Thirty years ago, America was considered the land of the brave and the free. Living in England at that time with my middle-class northern accent would literally have limited me to where I could work, who I would marry, and where I would live. Class and race discrimination was huge.

I learned my humanitarian ways from my dad. If there was a position available at his factory and four white men and one dark-skinned man applied, it was guaranteed the dark-skinned man would get the job. That is, if he had the appropriate qualifications for the job. The same would happen if four able-bodied men and one dis-abled man applied for a job. The disabled man would automatically get the job if he had the necessary skills and qualifications. Just like my father, I always took care of the underdog.

My depression grew stronger. Remember, I ran away from home at twenty-three years of age but unfortunately brought myself and my problems with me. I went to see a doctor, seeking medical advice. They did not think I had any problems that warranted on going medical or psychiatric care.

The main issue was when I was alone, all my demons came alive. My negative monkey mind literally paralyzed me. It was hard to get out of bed sometimes, especially if I had nothing planned. Mark was simply inept to help me.

Although there was something that did come to light. Some of the things I thought were wrong with me were just simply normal growing pains, because all my life, I had never had anyone to talk to. I never knew what was normal thinking compared to abnormal thinking. Remember, I am an only child. However, it is definitely not normal to plan how to depart from this world early.

At twenty-nine years, I was sick and tired of feeling like an empty shell. I had no idea who Anne really was. All I knew was Anne was a people pleaser; her wants and needs came last. I decided I was going to jump off a bridge or get my shit together.

Again, whenever I needed help, mysteriously, the right person would show up. Coincidence or divine intervention?

I got an appointment with a Christian counselor whose services were free for people with a low income. She probably got paid by the state. She was older than me by about ten years. She had a kind smile and I felt at ease in her presence. Her office was dark and the furniture very worn. As I entered the room, she invited me to sit down on a chair opposite her. She said, "What can I do for you?"

I proceeded to tell her the sob story of my childhood and what was happening presently in my life. She carefully listened to me and never interrupted.

At the end of my allotted time, she looked at me, and this is exactly what she said. "Stop watching the news, wake up in a morning, and be grateful for what you have and the daily union you have with God most people have to wait a lifetime for one such encounter."

My eyes grew larger than saucers, and I said in amazement, "God is the one communicating with me?"

"Yes," she said.

"I thought everyone had this daily union"

"Certainly not!" she said. "You are blessed." She further said, "I don't need to see you anymore. I have patients who really have problems and need my help."

I left her office a different woman. I felt special and privileged to have God in my life. I said to myself, "I am going to spend time with God and get to know Him." Little did I know the amazing service-oriented life He had in store for me.

CHAPTER 6

The Stork Delivered

I heard of this magnificent God in elocution lessons, Lady Bird books, and Sunday school. I always thought of God as out there and me over here. I thought He was unapproachable, too busy for the likes of me. However, without a doubt, someone or something had been looking out for me and guiding me throughout my life.

Now that I have brought the word *God* up, please don't put the book down. This is not a religious book. It is about being guided by a power greater than myself. This is about my personal relationship with God who has loved, guided, and protected me my whole life. In fact, if it were not for God, I would not have been able to write this book. I would be dead!

So you can substitute God for a power greater than yourself of your own understanding. It could be mother nature, universal energy, inner consciousness, or a world leader that you aspire to be like. However, in my case, nothing—let me say that again nothing—will ever replace the God of the Bible, the God that made the heaven and earth.

The next monumental episode in my life was the conversation with Mark about children. I was adamant I did not want any children. I was so ill-equipped to look after myself, let alone a baby. However, the universe, God, or mother nature decided differently.

Mark's older brother, his wife, and their three children decided to come for a visit. I never had so such fun in my life. We hired a car and at the back, there was a seat facing ongoing traffic. I sat in the middle of two of the children and we would wave at the cars behind us. We laughed and joked. We made the Hawaiian welcoming two-finger sign to onlookers. I was a happy kid again but with two awesome playmates.

After dinner, we would role-play. One performance was everyone had to pretend they drank poison and act out the dying scene. Of course, my act was the best, and those kids soaked up every minute of my dramatic death scene.

The children were aged ten, seven and four. We were all totally unaware of what the so-called "grown-ups" were doing. We lived in a dreamlike reality. Remember, as a child, I had an incredible imagination which I have kept all my life.

We took the family all over the place—San Francisco, Napa, and Yosemite. They were from Detroit, so the Californian scenery was breathtaking to them. When it was time for them to leave, I was heartbroken. However, we arranged for the eldest daughter to come back for another vacation very soon.

In fact, Julie, the eldest daughter, visited us for three years consecutively. We had so much fun walking, talking, swimming in the Doughboy in our backyard, and playing with Charlie.

After all those wonderful visits with Mark's family, I was ready to have a child. We tried for three months to get pregnant. The conception happened during a camping trip in Yosemite. We had the campsite to ourselves and we were running around naked and decided to do it on a big rock in the middle of the rushing river. Maybe that is too much information.

I asked God to give me an easy pregnancy, but in the delivery room, I did not care what happened as long as the baby was healthy. That was a big mistake with a capital B. I was now thirty-one years old. It was May 1991.

I had an amazing pregnancy, no morning sickness, and felt no difference physically from being pregnant and not being pregnant. God answered my prayers. What I found amazing was the baby hardly moved. I thought to myself, I am going to have a really calm and quiet baby. Boy, was I wrong.

The baby did not want to come into this world on my due date. About one week before I went into the hospital, I went for a doctor's visit and they did an ultrasound. The doctor was somewhat alarmed that there was not enough embryonic fluid between the baby and my stomach lining. He immediately scheduled a hospital appointment for the baby to be induced. I swore up and down if I had a Caesarean delivery with Nathan, I would have no more children.

They decided to bring me in the evening before the induction. However, they gave me morphine to sleep, and instead of sleeping, I vomited all night. When Mark came the next day, I simply looked like hell.

They started the induction, and I said to myself, "This is not too bad." Then after an hour, the torture began. I had contractions every two minutes for hours on end. The doctors told me to concentrate on a picture on the wall during the pain. I thought Mark would be useless helping me in anyway, because during all the Lamaze classes, he went to sleep. Probably the only husband that ever did that. I thought, *How embarrassing*.

During my pregnancy, I did not add an extra pound to any part of my face and body. All the weight went into my stomach. Sometimes it was hard to notice I was pregnant. In fact, during our last Lamaze class, Dr. Ruth gave us a visit. She went around the room, pointing at each woman, saying, "Your pregnant, your pregnant, your pregnant." And she stopped when she got to me and said, "Are you pregnant?"

Going back to the hospital room, Mark was amazing. He rubbed my back every two minutes during the contractions to help me get through the pain. At one point, the nursing staff gave me a sedative, and I proceeded to fall off the toilet several times onto the floor that night.

However, something bizarre happened approximately thirty hours into the induction. Nathan's heartrate had dropped to thirty beats a minute. They rushed me into the Emergency Room and prepped me for an emergency caesarean section. I signed the papers, and when the doctor was about to cut me open, he suddenly stopped, put the knife down, and told the nursing staff to put me back into my hospital room. Now this was Kaiser hospital, that simply does not happen. After thirty-seven hours—yes, you heard me right—I begged for an epidural and got one. I got some relief.

Almost two days had passed since I was admitted to the hospital. I lost count of all the doctors and nurses I had seen. Finally, a doctor arrived to save the day. He said angrily to the nursing staff, "Why is this woman still here after two days?" No one answered. He examined me and was quite rough, trying to get the baby to move. We did not know what the gender of the child was going to be, but everyone said it must be a boy. He was so stubborn. He didn't want to come out.

I was taken into the delivery room. The doctor got the baby to move down slightly, then he put a suction cup on its head and pulled and pulled like he was trying to open a wine bottle. There was a mirror overhead so I could see what was happening. Finally, the baby's head appeared, and then the rest of the body appeared. I was the first person to see the testicles, and I shouted, "It's a boy! It's a boy!" His head was shaped like a cone from the aggressive pulling by the doctor to get him out.

The doctor turned to Mark and said, "Your wife is one tough woman. She went through a lot."

They cleaned Nathan up, wrapped him, and placed him in my arms. Almost immediately, he turned his little head toward me and gave me the biggest stare. It was almost as if he was saying, "So that's what you look like."

I think it was the next morning we all went home. Now I was a new mother, with no family nearby to help and no experience with newborns. The opening of a new chapter in my life.

Just a quick note about strength and endurance. If someone had told me I would be in labor for fifty hours and all the other complications that occurred, I would have told you I was physically incapable of doing that. A favorite sentence of mine you will hear many times reading this book is, "God will do for you what you cannot do for yourself." He can give you supernatural power when it is necessary. I think that is amazing.

I bounced back very quickly after delivering Nathan, thank goodness. I think after one day, Mark went back to work. I got a big sinking feeling in my stomach. I did not want to be left alone. I breastfed Nathan, which was a real challenge. It seemed like I sat on the sofa for eight hours a day breastfeeding him. I did that for three months and then I quit.

Nathan was a beautiful baby with big deep brown eyes, and I could not stop hugging and kissing him. At three months old, he caught a bug and had constant diarrhea for over a week. I was exhausted. I remember turning to Nathan and saying, "I cannot do this anymore." He turned his head toward me and gave me his first big kiss. It melted my heart!

During that week of his illness, we moved to our second house. I felt lonely and isolated as a new mother. I had no family to talk to and no real close friends. Mark was always at work.

Nathan started running at nine months old and he wore me out. Thank goodness age was on my side. He also had a very curious mind and asked the most amazing questions for a little guy, like, "Why is the world round? Why does there have to be war?"

When Nathan was three months old, I returned to the cosmetics industry selling Biotherm. I also started videotaping weddings for a local photographer. It was really interesting going to the different venues. I continued doing that off and on, depending on my availability.

When Nathan was around two years old, Mark and I discussed about having another child. Although the little guy was keeping me going twelve hours a day, I swore I would never have an only child. I was not going to repeat what happened to me.

Looking at the whole picture, it was probably not a good idea. Mark would not let me take breaks after looking after Nathan all day, every day. I had no family to help out. I had joined a small mother's group where all the toddlers got together to play, but I never felt a part of that.

Ultimately, I really wanted to try for a girl. I got pregnant after three months of trying, and because I was thirty-five, I was offered an amniocentesis during the second trimester. The results showed I was having a girl. Hooray! Again, I had a perfect pregnancy, no morning sickness, and only put weight on around my stomach.

Every woman who has had more than one child says no two pregnancies are alike. Well, I must be an exception to the rule, because my pregnancies were identical. I had to be different. Are you surprised?

When I went to see my doctor for my final examination, before going into hospital to deliver Sarah, she told me I was already four centimeters dilated. She said this baby would come out with a couple of pushes and delivery would be very easy. I thought to myself, *Thank goodness.*

The day arrived and I went to the hospital to deliver Sarah. I was relaxed and hopeful this delivery would be a piece of cake. I was probably in the hospital room for around twenty hours, and still no baby. I finally went to sleep.

While I was sleeping, I was suddenly woken up and told the baby's heartbeat had fallen to thirty beats a minute—the exact same thing that happened with my last pregnancy. They rushed me down to the Emergency room for an emergency caesarean section. I was in a state of terror. They asked me to sign the consent form for the operation. I could hardly sign the paper because my hands were shaking so much.

On the operating table, the doctor, with the knife in hand, said, "Can you feel your legs?"

I screamed, "Yes, I can!"

The anesthesiologist administered some more medication, and the doctor asked me again, "Can you feel your legs?"

"Yes I can," I screamed. I thought. *Oh no, they are going to cut into me while I can still feel my legs!* So I proceeded to try and get off the operating table. They had to strap me down, and I don't remember anything else. I do remember regaining consciousness and seeing Sarah as they took her from me. I was horrified. She looked black. If they had waited one more second to cut into me, she probably would have had some brain damage. She was black from a lack of oxygen.

They pushed the gurney I was lying on into a corner of the room and left me there. I was shaking uncontrollably from the trauma of the operation and felt extremely cold. I had no idea how long I was lying there. Eventually, a doctor noticed me and asked the nursing staff, "Why is this woman alone, unattended to in the corner of the room?" They immediately brought what appeared to look like large aluminum sheets to warm me up.

When I finally was taken back to my hospital room, I went to sleep for quite a few hours. In the morning, Mark brought Nathan to see me and his new baby sister. I was hooked up to an intravenous drip and looked like I had been run over by a truck. They had me so heavily sedated I was frightened to hold Sarah in case I dropped her.

Nathan walked into my room with his stuffed toy rabbit, called Thumper, and said in a fearful voice, "Are you broken, Mommy?"

I replied, "Yes, I am, but I will mend quickly."

The nursing staff brought Sarah in so we could all see her. Both children weighed seven pounds, twelve ounces. Nathan looked at Sarah with great curiosity and I think he was wondering if she was coming home with us.

Unfortunately, I could not enjoy the whole new mother experience. I was in so much pain from the caesarean section. They had me on heavy pain medication.

I think I left the hospital a couple of days later. Mark took a week off work to help me out. This was going to be a long recovery. Constant pain, no driving, and no real outside support. When we brought Sarah home, she seemed to have a breathing problem, so we sat her upright in a laundry basket next to our bed so we could monitor her breathing.

I took some really adorable memorable pictures of Nathan holding Sarah. We were now a complete family.

It was hard for me to sit for long periods of time on the couch. I had so much nervous energy. I would describe myself at that time as very high-strung. It was hard for me to be in the moment for very long. I definitely had a monkey mind.

I videotaped everything the children did. I mean everything; I did not want to forget anything that happened. They grew so quickly. I took copious amounts of photographs. I thought, *When I get old and I am sitting in my rocking chair, looking at all these photographs and videos will occupy me for hours.*

After six weeks of recovery time and starting to drive again, I started organizing a routine for daily activities. One of my strengths is I like to be organized. I believe the day runs more smoothly when you schedule meals and outings.

When Sarah was born, Nathan was three and a half years old and he started going to preschool. I think he liked playing with other children. At the very least, it was a change of pace.

At three months old, Sarah started getting vocal and cried a lot. Nathan did not like the disturbance and said to me, "Mommy, can we take her back to the hospital?"

I replied, "No we cannot do that. She is here to stay."

Remember I mentioned if I had a caesarian section with Nathan, I was not going to have a second child? Do you remember the circumstances that happened around Nathan's delivery? Being in the Emergency Room and unexpectedly being put back into my room, even after thirty-seven hours of induction? Well, those events happened for a reason. Sarah was meant to be born no more than Nathan was meant to be born. But the chances of her ever being conceived were zero to nil if I had gone under the knife.

Makes you wonder, doesn't it? There must be a higher intelligence, a greater consciousness, or God who is in charge of all things. Maybe there have been circumstances in your life that you thought were just coincidences, but now maybe you have second thoughts. I love the mystical experiences in life. You cannot explain them. They just are!

CHAPTER 7

Listen Very Carefully to the Whisper

This next chapter is devoted to answered prayers and acts of service I undertook for God. I am highly intuitive and very sensitive to energies, good and bad. Let me tell you a story how one simple action motivated by God can literally change a chain of events in someone's life.

It was one weekend in May. I had rented a booth at a craft fair at Mankas Corner, Fairfield. After going on a vacation to Venice, I decided to try and sell Murano glass pendants and earrings handmade from Italy. The weather was overcast and the air was filled with the most pungent negative energy I have ever felt. I was full of anxiety and had a feeling of impending doom, the complete opposite energy to what I would normally feel when selling this jewelry. In fact, I would normally get really excited and consider a craft fair a special outing.

There were about eighty different retailers, and each booth was beautifully arranged with the different multicolored merchandise. Everyone was hustling to get everything perfectly displaced for the oncoming buyers. Mankas Corner is situated on the outskirts of Fairfield, surrounded by vineyards, large oak trees, open fields, and there is a sense of country living.

The first day of the event went at a slow but steady pace. The ladies loved placing the different pendants around their necks and looking at themselves in the mirror. When they found the perfect one, they would beam at their reflection in the mirror, puff their chest out like a proud peacock, and say, "I would like to buy this one, please." I would place the pendant ever so carefully in a blue box and then carefully slide it in a blue velvet bag. Presentation of the final purchase is extremely important, especially if it is a present for someone. As I mentioned before, I am a stickler for detail. You would definitely notice, if you met me, that I like to feel feminine and buy unique pieces of jewelry to add to my collection; and other women like to do the same.

I returned the next day to sell my jewelry. That awful energy was still present in the air. I really wanted to leave. I felt an evil presence of something. I kept looking around, trying to identify where it was coming from, but detected nothing.

It was around 2:00 p.m. on a Sunday afternoon, and the answer to my question was finally answered. A dark-skinned unkempt man walked into the scene. He looked like he was possessed by a demon, unable to control his outward mannerisms. He looked mentally disturbed. He was looking all around, trying desperately to find something that could comfort him.

He bought a beer and started drinking it. How interesting that he stuck out like a sore thumb but no one paid him any attention. He looked like he had not had a shower for a couple of days, and he looked unshaven. He actually frightened me, but I knew God had placed me at that event for a reason. I never approach people in his particular mental state. I consciously don't put myself in harm's way.

He was making his rounds and eventually came to my booth. The chaotic dark negative energy that came from that man made me want to run, but I knew I couldn't. Then suddenly, without any prompting, I grabbed hold of his hand and said in a commanding voice, "God loves you unconditionally, just the way you are." I was shocked. Where did that come from? I stood very still, anticipating what was going to happen next.

Almost simultaneously as I spoke those words, the dark energy lifted up and out of the man. I looked into his once tormented eyes and saw peace. He said very quietly, "Thank you." Wow, I knew I had to be an open vessel for God's energy to enter the man's body, but it was extremely difficult trying to stay composed.

The man left the event, and a peaceful energy was restored in the air. I had shared this experience with a clairvoyant, and he said the man had murderous intentions, but because of the intervention, no one was harmed. How interesting how the spiritual world works. Maybe sometimes in your life or mine, there was going to be a tragedy, but without you even knowing, your higher power had changed that course of events. God, who is most definitely my higher power, is always watching out for me because He knows the plans He has in store for my life and the life of others. We are all connected, and each one of us is a piece of the puzzle; without each piece, there cannot be a whole.

Shortly after Nathan was born, I opened my own wedding photography business. Everyone said, "You cannot do that, you have no formal training." No, I didn't have any schooling. I simply assisted a wedding photographer for a couple of weekends.

Now, I didn't know the working knowledge of a camera, but boy do I know how to see an image and put it on film. I was considered one of the best photographers around. I photographed weddings in the Napa and Sonoma wineries. I think I mentioned I like making people happy. I like providing services and making a mark on people's lives.

Wedding photography is extremely challenging, physically and mentally. I worked at a very fast pace. However, being high-strung, that pace of work was perfect for my temperament. I always give 110 percent effort in everything I do. I remember photographing a wedding in Calistoga, and the groom said, "I knew you were good, but I never imagined you were that good." I think that was the same groom that broke down and cried when I showed him his wedding pictures. He simply could not believe how good they were.

Now I did have a director during those weddings. Yes, it was God. I always wrote out timelines for the pictures I was going to shoot during the wedding day. I am detailed-oriented, remember? Let me give you a couple of examples when the schedule was rearranged.

I had scheduled to take some romantic pictures of a bride and groom at a particular spot at a particular time. I was instructed to change the timing because the sprinkler system would come on.

Always listen to Spirit, it will never lead you astray. I listened to God and photographed the couple at a different time, out of sheer trust, and yes, it would have been a complete disaster if I had stuck to my schedule. They would have gotten drenched with water.

The other most amazing memorable event was when I was photographing a wedding in Calistoga. Behind the gazebo where the wedding ceremony was held was a lake full of ducks, geese, and a couple of swans. After I had photographed all the formal family photographs and some reception shots, I would take what I call the "romantic shots." The lighting outside had to be a certain setting so the pictures had a warm soft glow. I wanted to take the bride and groom with the lake behind them with the wildlife, but all the wildlife had gone.

God instructed me to set up my camera pointing to the lake and to go get the bride and groom. As I posed the bride and groom for pictures, up in the sky were the geese and swans flying in a straight line. They landed in the lake and swam in a straight line right behind the bride and groom, the exact time I was taking photographs. The pictures were perfect. Wow, set an intention, ask in prayer, and wait. God does the rest, if it's his Will. If you don't ask, you don't get the gift.

Let's go back to life with my children. Nathan was now in third grade and Sarah was in kindergarten. They were both attending a Christian school in Fairfield.

Unexplainably, Nathan started crying at night. Something was happening at school. It had something to do with the teacher picking on him. At the same time, Sarah was having problems. The teacher said she was not paying attention. Come on, she was only four years old and had lots of energy!

Mark and I made an appointment to see Nathan's teacher. She started complaining about Nathan's hair. Everybody in the family has naturally curly hair. Mark's ancestry was from Sicily. I alarmingly said, "His hair is annoying you so you pick on him? And you are the pastor's wife!"

She did not directly answer the question but insinuated that was the problem. Now I knew I must have misunderstood the answer, so

I asked the question again. She again said his hair really annoyed her. That was all I needed to hear. We were paying good money for our children to go to this school. I will talk about Christians later in this book. Right now, I want to continue with my story.

I went home and prayed earnestly that God would help me move my children to another school. However, all too often, we have a preconceived idea how prayer should be answered, and I certainly did. Remember, I was in my thirties and ashamedly, I have to admit I fought with God. Thank goodness God has patience with all His children. Stubbornness runs in my immediate family, my parents' family, and Mark's ancestry. Now I didn't actually say that, did I? I am stubborn!

God directed me to BSF (Bible Study Fellowship) in Vacaville. I simply could not understand why. This large group of women, sometimes over a hundred ladies, started a new Bible study once a year. I protested. "No, I am not going to attend." I behaved like a spoiled child at Christmas not getting everything she wanted on her Santa list. I was having a tantrum.

God's reply was, "Yes, you will attend."

We fought back and forth. Something I say today is, "Tell God your plans so you can give him a good laugh."

I remember the day the Bible study started. It was going to be held in a church in Vacaville. I walked into the church, stomping my feet with a grimace on my face.

"Well," I said to God, "I am here. What now?"

I sat down and listened to the orientation. They were then going to separate the 100 plus ladies into groups of eight. We got together in our individual groups and introduced ourselves. In my particular group was the administration officer for a Christian school in Vacaville. I told her I was planning to send Nathan there the next year. She replied, "You will never get him in. Registration for fourth grade gets full before the public has a chance to register any student. Also, third grade right now is full. No one is leaving."

I always wear my emotions on my sleeve. She then proceeded to ask me if I had any other children. I said, "Yes, I have a little girl in kindergarten."

She suggested I move Sarah over to the school immediately, then I would have a chance to register Nathan in fourth grade before it was open to the public.

So I moved Sarah from the old school to the new one. I went into the office of the new school where I had just met the administration officer in BSF and signed all the necessary papers to enroll Sarah. I told Cynthia (the administration officer) that I was going to come back in one week and she was going to tell me someone was going to leave third grade.

She said, "It is February. No one is going to leave before the end of this semester. I would have been told by now."

I walked into the new school one week later with my head held high. I looked straight into Cynthia's eyes and asked, "Well, is someone leaving third grade?"

She replied, "Yes, someone is."

I simply said, "God would not let my son down."

Within four weeks of following God's direction and having faith, both my children had moved to a new school, and everyone was happy. God is amazing!

Now I don't know if you are familiar with the nursery rhyme *The King Has No Clothes*. Well, it is about a group of swindlers who come to town to try and sell the king a magnificent handmade suit of clothes. They tell the king, "It is made with the highest quality fabric, and if you cannot see it, you are a fool."

The king, not wanting to appear a fool, agrees with the swindlers and buys the suit. The whole town goes along with the idea. Of course, there is no suit.

When the king walks through the town, everybody cheers and tells him how magnificent he looks. However, there is a small boy in the crowd who shouts out, "The king has no clothes on."

Well, I am just like the little boy. I am not going to go along with popular opinion. I have a mind of my own and say what I see and think, regardless of what people might say. One of the gifts God gave me was to see the truth in outside situations. However, my broken inner child could not allow me to see the truth in my personal relationships. In fact, I was not ready for that awakening at this time of my life.

We went to a local church every Sunday as a family. The pastor, during his service, would always talk about himself. He did this and he did that. His ego was always talking. The message should be that God empowered him to accomplish the task in hand, just like God is empowering me to write this book.

Well, one Sunday, I took it upon myself to tell him his ego was getting in the way of his message. He was furious. In fact, he asked one of his high-ranking Christian women who attended the church to cross-examine me. I agreed to the challenge. I met with her several times that week to talk about God.

I know some of you are thinking I was out of line talking to the pastor like that, but I honestly look at things with a childlike spirit. I had lived my life with God in a sort of bubble. I had not yet learned I needed to censor my voice in certain situations.

At the end of my interrogation, the woman said, "It was an honor and privilege speaking with you. You are the real deal."

It got me wondering. I guess to outsiders I must appear somewhat egotistical, especially when I say God talks to me. Well, like Jesus says in Mark 6:11, NIV, "And if any place will not welcome you or listen to you, leave that place and shake the dust off your feet as a testimony against them." Spirituality can be very confusing to some people. Hopefully reading this book will give you some tools to use to help you navigate through your life.

The next two stories are examples of how God downloads information to me, and I just follow his instructions, no questions asked.

Sarah was in third grade at the Christian school in Vacaville. God told me to go buy the book called *The Praying Wife* (I was not familiar with the book) and a candle and give it to Sarah's third grade teacher. I did what He asked and proceeded to go to knock on the door of the classroom where I knew the teacher was preparing for class.

As she opened the door, I gave her the book and the candle. She looked at me in amazement and said, "How did you know my husband went to war today?"

I said, "I didn't. But God knew. I am just following His instructions."

That year, the classroom had a Christmas party, and at the party, the third grade teacher said something about each mother whose child was in her class. When she got to me, she said, "Mrs. Hayes' timing is always impeccable. She knows what to do at the exact right time."

What she should have said—but then again it could have been misunderstood—was, "Mrs. Hayes always follows God's instructions exactly the moment she receives them."

As a result of me giving the book called *The Praying Wife* to Sarah's teacher, it proved to be so powerful in her life. She bought the book for all the mothers of the children in her class. She gave all the credit to me, but she shouldn't have. All the glory should go to God. I just followed instructions.

So another lesson I would like you to note is when you listen to God or a power greater than yourself, you have no idea what the ripple effect will do for the whole. One single act could affect hundreds of peoples' lives. So step out of your comfort zone and be the warrior God or your higher power intended you to be.

The second event that occurred was with another of Sarah's teachers. This time, the information was not well received. I told this teacher, "Something close to you has died."

She responded, "A child of mine died, but there is no way you could have known that."

I then told her, "God wants you to give up your anger or you will get cancer."

She then proceeded to tell me she was a cancer survivor. I was then going to tell her what a gifted teacher God thought she was, but she ran away out of sheer fear. Another lesson to note: we are not responsible for the outcome of an event, only responsible for planting the seed and being obedient to spirit.

Now let me tell you a couple of fun stories that I tell anybody who will listen, even if I have already told them three times before.

Sarah was about five or six years old. I took her to the chamber of commerce monthly meeting. They had food and raffle prizes. We bought some raffle tickets because it was always fun to try and win something. We enjoyed a fun evening, sampling food and chocolate desserts. Then at the end of the meeting, they started the raffle. Sarah spotted a giant long stuffed toy crocodile. It was about five to six feet long, and she really wanted it.

In front of all the people who were gathered around for the raffle, about eighty business owners, Sarah got down on her knees and prayed to God to win the crocodile. She had her hands tightly clasped together in prayer and her face was full of conviction and sincerity. The raffle tickets were drawn, and to Sarah's disappointment, she did not win. A woman stepped up and claimed the prize and walked around the corner out of sight. I followed her and said, "My daughter prayed to win that crocodile. Can I buy it from you?"

She hesitantly agreed. I gave her $25 and took the toy crocodile, and as I gave it to Sarah, I said, "God answers all honest sincere prayers, but not always the way you expect."

To see Sarah's face when I gave her the crocodile was priceless! It was probably not the right thing to do insisting on buying the crocodile from the woman, but unfortunately, I was very codependent those days. I was always the people pleaser, especially to my children. A limiting belief developed at childhood. If I please you, you will love me. Not true.

The next story, which is etched in my memory, was when I went on a field trip with Nathan to go gold panning near Sonora with his school. It was a beautiful day. We travelled on a coach to our destination. There were at least fifty students, and they were laughing and giggling with excitement in anticipation for the outing. Somewhere along the way, Nathan bought a glass Indian arrow. It became his prized possession. He kept taking it out of his pocket and looking at it.

It was an amazing day. The kids panned for gold in a man-made trove. It was a great memory seeing them delight in seeing the gold flakes in their pans. After lunch, we travelled to a cave and went down multiple stairs to get to the bottom. We had flashlights. It was extremely dark at the bottom. The teacher instructed us to turn our flashlights off and the children began to sing. It sounded like a chorus of angels singing praises to the Lord. I had goosebumps all over my body. A wave of complete peace came over my entire body. I experienced heaven on earth. I did not want to leave, but alas, it was time to go home.

On the way home, all the parents were exhausted, but the children were still full of the excitement from the day. Nathan went to the bathroom on the coach, and as he left the bathroom, the door slammed closed onto his Indian arrowhead which he had in his hand. The arrowhead dropped to the floor and broke in half. He came back to his seat with the two pieces, and the look on his face broke my heart.

We were now one hour out of the Gold Country, and the chances of finding another arrowhead were zero to nil. However, I know from experience that with prayer, nothing is impossible. So I started praying, asking God for an Indian arrowhead.

The teacher instructed us we were going to stop for pizza. As the coach approached the pizza parlor, I saw an Indian store. What was an Indian store doing an hour out of the Gold Country and standing alone all by itself?

It was a hundred degrees outside. I asked Nathan, "Do you want to run to the store?" It was about a quarter of a mile away. He said yes, so off we went. I remember the sweat pouring down my face, and my face was beet red.

I rushed into the store and asked the man behind the counter, "Do you have an Indian arrowhead?"

He replied, "No."

By now, I was hot, tired, thirsty, and very hungry, so I said in an angry manner, "Get out of my way." I started searching all the merchandise in the cabinets. By the time I got to the back of the store and the last counter, there it was! A metal Indian arrowhead! I told the cashier, "I want to buy that arrowhead." I bought it and left the store.

As soon as we walked out of the store, I turned to Nathan and said, "Here you are!"

He looked at me and was speechless. Then he looked straight into my eyes and said, "You're amazing, Mom." He simply could not comprehend what happened.

I said, "God is good."

We ran back to the pizza parlor and finally we got something to eat.

I was very grateful to be able to be a stay at home Mom. I got to go to all their activities. Then in the summer months, I would work on the weekends as a wedding photographer.

Life was really good. How could anything go wrong? Well, as they say, "life can turn at a dime." The next episode of my life was by far the hardest. Are you ready to read the story? You might want to take some deep breaths. I certainly need to.

CHAPTER 8

Nothing Lasts Forever

This book is not a religious book, but it is spiritual in nature. It is meant to help you bring awareness and meaning to your life. It is a roadmap for your journey through life. It is a book meant to inspire hope and encourage you to help humanity in whatever way you can. If we do not change our value system from control and selfishness to love and service to others, our planet will die.

Some of our greatest spiritual teachers of today predict the world will only survive another 150 years. That means our children's children will have nowhere to live and simply die.

I was instructed by God to write this book. I have put no expectations on the outcome. God is in charge of that. I plant the seed, He waters it and helps it grow.

Let's get back to my journey.

It was now around the year 2000. Life was good in America, especially in California, the Golden State.

I had been married for almost seventeen years. The children were growing up fast. Over the years, Mark had become more and more financially successful. As well as growing his business, he had managed to build a couple of houses. He was a workaholic, and even when he was physically home, he was never home. He had become egotistical, prideful, and greedy. Nothing was enough. He needed more and more. The seven deadly sins are not called deadly for no reason. Anything you crave outside of yourself—money, food, alcohol, or work—becomes your god. It takes on a life of its own; it literally changes the neuropathways in your brain.

You think filling the desires of your flesh will mend your broken inner child. That miraculously, you will look like someone of value to the outside world. You become judgmental of others so you can feel superior. Everyone around is doing the same thing. Surely this is the answer to the riddle of life.

I hope to enlighten you that choosing the spiritual path may not give you instant gratification but will develop within you a soundness of mind, a sense of purpose, and a need to help grow a healthy community around you. You can transform from survival mode to living in the present moment with peace, knowing your higher power is omnipresent and is continually guiding and protecting you. I simply could not live my life without God.

I started to feel lonely. Mark practically was gone from early in the morning to late at night. I even asked him if he had a wife and family in another town.

I want to mention briefly about the five languages of love. Although Mark and I both came from dysfunctional families, our language of love was very different. I needed hugs and kisses, words of encouragement, and quality time.

Mark, on the other hand, couldn't care less about those things. His language of love was acts of service and gifts. One of his addictions was thinking. Now where did I mention that before with another man who was prominent in my life?

He was so detached from people, he had no idea how his actions affected others. It got to a point where when he got home from work, neither myself nor the children even turned our heads in his direction. He mentioned that he thought we would never miss him if he never came home. He was right. We wouldn't.

There is no family unity today. People don't eat dinner together, everyone isolates themselves. The cell phone is the new addition; people cannot put them down. Again, their brains get rewired. When people get married, the minister conducting the ceremony should say, "Do you take this man and his cell phone as your lawful husband?" The cell phone literally destroys relationships; it did in my case.

It took prevalence over me all the time. Depending on the message from the person on the either end of the phone, it can destroy a beautiful moment in time. Again, what is your value system? I could literally get in a hot tub with Mark and he would move as far away from me as possible so he could be in his head. When we were in Italy on a ferry at Lake Como, he deliberately went to the other side of the ferry so he could be by himself; and we were on vacation! Now I don't want to be prideful, but I am beautiful, have a lively personality, and I'm in good physical shape. He has been known to hear the words *you have it all* from others. Even when we went out to parties, as soon as we started mingling with others, I simply did not exist anymore. That old core wound kept being solidified over and over again. I am not lovable or he would not want to leave me alone. So to dull my feelings of inadequacy, what did I do? Yes, I went to search out the wine bottle.

After a couple of glasses of wine, I got to the point that I could not care less. I always got attention at parties, but you can be rest assured if I started getting too much attention from the male species, Mark would suddenly appear. He would puff his chest out like a gorilla and make sure everyone knew I was his property.

So one morning, when I was in the kitchen making coffee, Mark walked in and said, "Why do you pray to your God when I am god?"

I became very still and fearful because I knew he had just set the ball in motion for disaster. I said, "Now you've done it. See what my God does to you now." God will simply not allow anyone to treat me badly or disrespect me concerning my faith.

During my marriage, I never thought for one second that I would never want to not be married to Mark. I thought we would be buried in the same casket when we both died. I cannot tell you when I made this decision, but it was not long after our conversation in the kitchen. I asked God in a small still voice under my breath, "Get me out of this marriage." Be careful what you ask for, because you never know how God is going to answer your prayer.

It was now September 2001, and on the eleventh of the month, we tragically had the attack in New York. I remember exactly where I was when I heard the news. I was driving the children to school and we were at the last traffic light before turning into the school entrance. It was on the news and it seemed surreal. I think I went into shock and I remember starting to cry.

I parked my car in the school parking lot and walked Sarah to her classroom. Nathan went by himself to his destination. I was now sobbing uncontrollably but noticed no one around me had even skipped a beat in their normal routine. Everyone was walking around the school grounds like ants trying to hurry to their destination. No one else was crying. Everyone and everything looked exactly the same as it normally did during the morning hours at school. This intensified my fears. What was going on? I thought I must have misunderstood what I heard on the news. After Sarah had safely gotten to her classroom, I went back to my car and drove home.

When I got home, I put on the news and, yes, what I had heard was correct. I sat on the couch and started rocking back and forth. I looked like a psychiatric patient in a mental ward. I could not have been any more devastated if you told me my two children had died.

Mark walked into the room. He never consoled me. He simply said, "Get yourself together, we have to go to a car dealership and buy a car."

I said, "Are you kidding me? Have you seen what is happening in New York?"

Now this is typical Mark. It doesn't matter if the world is coming to an end. If Mark has decided to do something at a certain time on a certain day, it will be done. He was like a machine or, should I say, the Energizer bunny. He went on and on every day, completing all the tasks he had put on his to-do list that morning, expressing only anger if he couldn't stay on target.

We went to the car dealership and surprise, we were the only customers there. He looked at all the vehicles he was interested in and then we came home. It never seemed to bother him what was going on in New York.

I cannot tell you what an eerie feeling it is when I am falling apart and others are going through their day undisturbed. It is like being in the Twilight Zone. That was the first time it really got my attention, how out of touch Mark was with reality and his lack of need to comfort me.

In October of the same year, we had planned a trip to Sicily. I had gotten a travel book and put together a two-week vacation travelling around the country. Now I had prayed to God a couple of years before to allow me to have at least one amazing vacation with my husband. All previous vacations always seemed to have "a bump in the road."

The trip to Sicily was amazing. Everything went smoothly. Mark and I were totally in sync with one another. The country was breathtaking, accommodation was superb, and every night, Mark and I would sit together eating, drinking, talking, and you can guess the rest.

We could not speak a single word of Italian, so I communicated with gestures and facial expressions. It worked out perfectly. Everyone understood exactly what I needed. I hope someday to go back to Sicily. However, just to warn you, Sicilians are crazy drivers. We rented a car and I would only do the driving. Just to give you an example of what I am talking about when you are driving along a road, someone may try to overtake you, which is usual. However, it is not usual for someone else to be overtaking the car that is overtaking you. That can happen on the other side of the road also. So virtually six cars can be parallel with each other at any given time. Also, they drive one inch behind your bumper. There is absolutely no room for error.

I remember being in Palermo, sitting on the sidewalk, drinking coffee. There was a man driving his motorcycle with his girlfriend on the back. He tongue-kissed her as he was riding past me and continued tongue-kissing her through the traffic lights and around the corner. Crazy behavior from our point of view, but not from their culture.

After returning from the vacation and feeling on top of the world, I got a message from God. He said I was going to be brought to my knees. Sometimes, it is possible to misunderstand a message, but in this case, I knew for certain I had not misinterpreted it.

From my personal experience, when a message comes from God, it comes right out of the blue. It is also short in length, not wordy. The message usually causes a sensation throughout your whole body. I was so devastated by the news I told a couple of my girlfriends and asked myself, "Is this a message telling me I am going to die?" I started thinking about all kinds of different scenarios. However, that was a waste of time. I had to just wait.

We had planned to go to Detroit for Christmas and visit Mark's cousin and family. I was so excited! We had always spent Christmas by ourselves. Mark's cousin was also planning a family reunion for us so we could meet all the family.

I packed everybody's clothes and the Christmas gifts for everyone. When we arrived, it was snowing. Everything looked like a picture-perfect postcard. When we entered the house, the most unusual thing happened. Mark, myself, Nathan, and Sarah almost instantaneously seemed to meet individually our best friend. Mark and his cousin's husband were one of a kind. Myself and his cousin instantly bonded. Nathan and their son, as soon as they met each other, they disappeared into a bedroom and we never heard a peep out of them the entire week. Sarah bonded with the daughter. We had never seen or spoken to each other before that day, but it was as if we had known each other for years.

After a couple of days getting settled in Detroit, it was time for the family reunion. Now you know how Italian families are, there are lots of people. The complete opposite to how my family lived, isolated and alone.

It was very exciting and overwhelming to meet all the people. All the names and how they were related to each other was so confusing. I am not very good at remembering names to begin with.

It was time for Mark to make a speech. I anticipated him introducing me as his wife, and then the children. That never happened. All he did was talk about himself. In fact, even though I was standing close to him, he just completely ignored me. He never once mentioned our children. Then he proceeded to show everyone the pictures of the house that he had built. I told him not to do that because most of his relatives were poor, and we needed to stay humble and not brag about what we had. Mark's head got more and more inflated. I wanted to disappear into the floor. *What a jerk*, I thought to myself.

Then I got triggered by my old core beliefs. I am invisible and, of course, unlovable because I wasn't worth mentioning to the family. I got real quiet and started listening very carefully to what Mark was saying to his relatives. I realized I didn't have any value outside of what I could provide for Mark, being a trophy wife and taking care of the family. I also listened to the ongoing conversations between Mark's cousin and her husband. He was so disrespectful to her and acted like a spoiled child. He never held her in high esteem. Their conversations were exactly like the conversations Mark and I had, but this time I was looking from the outside in.

Mark simply only loved himself and no one else. How I describe what happened that day is "God took the rosy colored glasses off my face." All the denial and pain I had pushed way down deep inside came to the surface. The man I thought I loved now represented my father—a control freak, emotionally unavailable, self-centered, and angry inside. How the ego in a person sets up a false sense of reality in order to protect itself from experiencing pain! The ego is always self-serving and can be very devious to the point of becoming dangerous in telling lies and manipulating others to serve it's self-centered needs.

I simply could not wrap my mind around what had happened. How could I come to Detroit a happy woman and be leaving a devastated one? I tried to tell myself I was having a nightmare and I would wake up. Why was this so-called awakening affecting me so much? My intellectual mind could simply not override my primitive mind. The pain trapped in a person's body from trauma when activated can lead to life-threatening situations.

When we got home to California, I told Mark how I felt. He wasn't able to hear what I was saying. I told him I needed some help or something bad was going to happen. I felt like I was heading for a nervous breakdown.

What did the future hold? Please help me, God!

CHAPTER 9

When One Door Closes, Another One Opens

E very day, I lived in a state of despair and loneliness. Once, every day was a joy, and fulfilling my motherly tasks was not a chore. Now everything was drudgery and draining. I grew to resent Mark. I had been by his side for eighteen years, supporting him emotionally and taking care of the household. I had been the children's main support and now I felt I was inadequate to take proper care of them.

I talked to Mark for over a year trying to tell him that his constant preoccupation with making money had to stop. I was lonely and needed his help. I simply did not know where to turn for support. The best way to describe how I felt was standing on the edge of a cliff and someone was going to push me off. My heart was racing all the time.

In August of 2002, it was our wedding anniversary. I always celebrated everything—birthdays, Christmases, and wedding anniversaries. I remember we went to Sacramento for dinner and before we went into the restaurant, I got a passer-by to take a couple of pictures of us. I always recorded events with photographs. They always bring back the memories of that day. I was still using film in my camera at that time, so as soon as I was able, I took the film into Costco to be developed.

When I picked the photographs up, I was anticipating seeing the pictures from our wedding anniversary. Every picture on the roll of film came out except those two pictures from our special day. When I held the film up to the light to see if accidentally they were not developed, the two squares representing the two pictures were totally black. That means the pictures were taken but no image was captured. Without a doubt, I got the message.

Now this is very important information for the women reading this book. I had simply put all my eggs in one basket. I had relied on Mark for everything and trusted him in every sense of the word. We did not even have a joint bank account, so I had no idea how much money we had. As I said previously, I never thought there would be a day that I no longer wanted to be married. He had made sure that I did not have a good support group. I was like Rapunzel in the castle.

He was very clever in knowing how to control me. He used the same triggers as my parents. He told me I was unintelligent and that if I ever left him I would be homeless, sitting in a doorway, and be mentally disturbed. He also said he would never let me be with another man. He would kill me first. I really believed every word, which today people have a hard time believing I could have been that naïve.

Please know that those core wounds, limited beliefs and learned behaviors are so powerful that unless some kind of awareness happens, we are totally powerless over them. Even praying to God cannot miraculously release us from the bondage.

So having no money, no family, no outside support, nowhere to go, I decided to turn to drinking. I had always drunk a couple of glasses of wine every night, but now I turned to vodka. I was no longer drinking to just relax. I was drinking to forget my reality.

How pitiful. My shame and guilt increased around my drinking. I felt hopeless and helpless.

I never once put together the message from God that I was going to be brought to my knees with my drinking. When tragedy strikes, it is impossible to look at the big picture, although God is always in control.

Any addiction will eventually lead you to insanity, and by 2003, I was a full-blown alcoholic. I simply could not go a day without drinking. From 2002 to 2003, I had been secretly drinking vodka every night and getting really drunk. When I eventually told Mark, his reaction was, "I never knew you were drinking."

I was sleeping in the same bed with him every night. How could he not have known I was drunk? Again, I asked myself, "Am I living in an invisible bubble? Can no one see me?"

I actually grew to hate Mark, but he was no different than me. He was a workaholic and his drug was money. His addiction also made him completely disconnected from reality. He was also mentally ill. He rationalized in his head that having had no problems with me for eighteen years, I must be just going through a phase. I kept wishing that was the case.

My poor children. The mother they had grown to love and solely rely on was now falling apart. I did most of my drinking in the house at night, so my children were the ones who witnessed my downfall firsthand. I tried to keep it a secret to the outside world.

Writing this chapter is extremely hard because I am experiencing all the emotions once again. I took a five-minute break and asked God for some guidance through the Bible. I first prayed and then trusted God that I would open the Bible to the exact page He would want me to read. I opened at Song of Songs, verse 7, the power of love. It talks about how devotion and commitment were the main keys to Solomon and his wife's marriage. The message told me my marriage would never have sustained a lifetime, because there was no true love or commitment between Mark and myself.

Mark loved himself and was committed to making money, his family came second. Remember, I married Mark for my green card, the wrong motive in the first place for marriage. Anything you try and do with the wrong motive will be built on quick sand, and when the worldly winds come, the house blows down.

The next significant episode in my life was when we got a gopher in our backyard. The creature was tearing up the lawn. I don't know if this was part of God's plan. Everyone would say absolutely not, but I had to contact a varmint control contractor. When he came over, I could not help notice his kind blue eyes. He set up a trap to catch the gopher. When he came back a couple of days later, there was no gopher in the trap. It seemed to have miraculously left. I talked to him for a good half an hour, and he must have sensed my nervousness because when he left, he told me I could call him anytime. We talked for over a year. My hiking partner at that time said the guy helped to balance me out emotionally. After one year of communicating, I agreed to meet him at his place. I started having an affair, something I swore I would never do.

So in January 2005, I went to my first rehab. I really wanted to stop drinking. I wanted my old self back. I wanted to be joyful again. I had lost any sense of self-respect. The family came to visit me on the weekend. I don't know if you know anything about addiction, but no one can make you take the first step of a twelve-step recovery program. It is mandatory to honestly and wholeheartedly admit to oneself, "I am powerless over alcohol and my live has become unmanageable."

The dilemma is we drink or do some other form of addiction, because we are in fear, and our amygdala is always in a state of flight, fight, or freeze. We feel we need to defend ourselves and survive from impending doom or even death. It is an automatic survival instinct set up by the body. The process can only be interpreted by tragic circumstances implemented by God or a power greater than yourself or your own understanding. So in between using and taking that first step, anything can happen. The only thing you can do if you have loved ones in the same situation is simply pray for them. Prayer changes everything if it is God's will. Remember, if you don't ask, you will not receive.

I went to rehab for my family's sake. If I had been honest with myself, I was not done with drinking. I was still going to go back to my old circumstances in the house.

Mark found out about my affair through my phone bill. I didn't hide the fact I had been seeing someone else. Mark's reaction was not what I had expected. He seemed jealous, not from the fact I was seeing someone else, but jealous he had not experienced the so-called excitement from an affair himself.

That night, he asked me if I had the chance to see the guy again, would I? I knew I was supposed to say no if I wanted to protect myself, but I said yes out of pure spite. Mark went crazy, hitting me several times and breaking furniture in the bedroom. Both of us had been drinking heavily that night. I called 911 because I thought he was going to kill me. The police did arrive, but Mark told them there had been a mistake. I simply could not get up to go outside the bedroom to ask them for help.

The next day, I had bruises on my legs the size of a football. Mark never acknowledged anything happened that night.

A week later, when things had calmed down, he came up with a great idea. He said, "I think we should go to wife swapping parties. You will really enjoy it." I may have been an out of control alcoholic, but I saw how his devious mind was working. He really wanted to sleep with other women and use me as porn. In fact, I had no idea if he had already done so in the past. Remember, he was gone all the time.

I was really angry, because first, I was the mother of his children; and second, I was literally dying from alcoholism. Who takes advantage of someone in that state?

One of the most frightening things was I thought I knew my husband, but in actuality, I did not know him at all. You really don't know anyone until the chips are down. Sometimes another person's brokenness is just too bad to help anyone else, especially if they are not spiritually fit.

I started going to a twelve-step program, got a sponsor, and started working the steps. The problem was I was not being honest. I thought I could do the program my way. I was different, don't you know? Eight times out of ten, I could drink just a couple of drinks and then stop. However, the other two times was like Russian Roulette. You didn't know what was going to happen. I was able to somewhat carry on this charade for a couple of months.

I never realized how powerful alcoholism could be. I started drinking alcohol before I went to meetings, thinking no one would know. Right! A group of recovering alcoholics would not know that I was drinking! Sometimes they had to literally carry me into a meeting and carry me out. They sometimes took my car keys away from me and drove me home.

One terrifying event that happened when I was active in my disease was when I decided to clean the house one day. I thought, before starting the task, I would have a couple of drinks. I must have blacked out and called Chris's brother in Detroit, saying all kinds of crazy things on the phone. I must also have mentioned I wanted to harm myself because suddenly, without warning, seven ambulance men came through the front door, put me on a gurney, and rushed me to hospital. The next thing I remember was waking up in a hospital bed, strapped down, and a guard by my side. I had been admitted 51/50 (to prevent me from hurting myself). This unfortunate incident happened another two times. I remember the guard standing next to my bed saying, "Why don't you just stop drinking?"

The present house we were living in was a rental because we had sold our family house. Unfortunately, the owners of this rental house put the house up for sale, and when it was sold, we were asked to move out. We found another rental around the corner, but how in the world was I going to be able to pack all our things up and move to a different house when I was drunk every day?

Ten days before we were scheduled to move, there was a knock on the door. When I opened the door, their stood a couple of Mormon missionaries. They asked me if I needed any help.

I said, "Sure I do, I am an alcoholic. I am drunk every day and I need to pack up all my things to get ready to move."

They said, "No problem, we can help you do that."

"What?" I remarked. "You will help me do that?"

They replied "Yes."

I was totally flabbergasted.

They came into the house, helped me pack, and on the day of the move, twenty Mormons showed up and moved all our furniture. They then processed the next week to help me unpack all my things. Once everything was in order, more or less, they simply disappeared. Now how do you explain that? God was always protecting me, even when I was in my disease.

The poor children, they were trying to find all my jewelry and hide it from me so I would not sell it for alcohol. They must have been so scared. At times, my daughter had to put me in the bath and bathe me and wash my hair.

According to my mother, Mark had called them and was telling them what a bad person I was and that they needed to disown me and leave all their money to him. My father said, "I know my daughter, and if she is doing those things, she was driven to it."

Mark called all the people I knew and did the same thing, telling them what an awful person I was and they should never talk to me again. He wanted nobody to be on my side. He wanted everybody to turn their backs on me.

I had been married to him for twenty-one years by now. I had supported him emotionally while he built his business. I gave him two children. I was a very good wife and mother, and this is how he treated me. He wanted me to die so he did not have to share the wealth when we divorced.

It was now around September 2005, and I started thinking about Christmas and buying presents for the children. I did not want anything for myself. Again, as I mentioned before, I had never had a joint bank account with Mark, so I had no access to any money. He would not give me any money to buy the presents, so I had to sell my fidelity funds. When you take funds out early, you have to pay a big penalty. Mark did not care. It was hard to fathom I was married to such a mean-spirited man. Now I was not staying in "my box" and playing his game, he had absolutely no use for me.

By now, I was at the liquor store at 6:00 a.m. every morning. I would chug the vodka down in the parking lot and drive home. Thank goodness I was not driving my children around anymore. I had no idea at times how I got home. I was living every day in terror and could not live a day without drinking.

I was physically and mentally deteriorating. Clumps of hair were literally going down the shower drain. I was slowly dying and people around me felt powerless. The people in my twelve-step recovery group, Mark, and probably my children were anticipating my death.

Mark took away my car keys and my purse with all my money in it. But that didn't stop me from getting my alcohol. When everyone had left the house in the morning, I walked to the store to get my vodka.

I was so embarrassed going up to the cashier at 6:00 a.m. in a morning with my bottle of vodka. I looked like a homeless person. I wore the same dress every day and smelt terrible. Every pore in my body was sweating. You could smell me ten feet away. I wore a wool hat and tried to pull it down over my face to hide my bloodshot eyes. I tried to go to a different cashier each morning, hoping they did not recognize me as a regular.

I would literally go home and sit on the couch and stare at the walls for eight hours. I felt like I was living in hell. I remember one morning going to my bedroom and making an attempt to make my bed. I sat on the bedroom floor for two hours but simply could not complete that simple task.

It was now January 26, 2006. Having run out of money, I had to devise a plan. I remembered a check someone had written me and I had hidden it in my bedroom. I told the neighbor across the street I had locked my keys in my car and needed to go to the bank and then to the grocery store. He obliged me by driving me there. At this time, I was unable physically to walk any distance.

I went to the bank and cashed the check and then went to the store and bought three bottles of vodka. My daughter always found my vodka bottle and poured it down the sink, with three bottles, I could hide them all over the house.

When I returned to the house, I immediately opened one bottle of vodka, and by 4:00 p.m., had drank it all. I had gone into a blackout and apparently went into my bedroom and slammed my eye against the door. I developed a lump the size of a golf ball. I went to sleep that night, praying the misery would stop and that I would not wake up again.

Alas, morning came and the craving for alcohol was strong. I decided to go to the bathroom before hunting for my second hidden vodka bottle. As I passed by the mirror to go to the toilet, I glanced at myself. Who was that woman staring back at me? It couldn't be me.

Or was it? I looked like a cancer survivor with very little hair. My eyes were sunken, they weren't blue anymore, and I had a big black eye. It was like looking at a dead person or someone on the brink of death. My skin was grey and lifeless. Someone dies every three seconds from addiction around the world, and I would simply be another statistic.

I walked slowly into the bathroom, and as I came out I slipped. The fall seemed to last forever. I said to myself, "When my head lands on the hard tile floor, my life is going to change forever."

I also heard the words, "I am not going to drink again." I felt a sense of complete surrender, a kind of peace.

When my head landed on the tile floor, it split open. I laid lifeless in a pool of blood on the bathroom floor, and my soul should have finally left my body and gone to my creator. That should have been the end of my life that day, but it was actually the beginning of a new life that was to be divinely guided by God.

CHAPTER 10

Hazard, Pot Holes Ahead

I woke up in the hospital. I have no idea how I got there. The doctor said I should never have lived. I was admitted with a blood alcohol content of 0.4 percent. I had not drunk any alcohol that morning, so I probably went to bed the night before with a 0.5 percent blood alcohol content. The legal content is 0.08 percent. I should not have lived, but God had other plans.

I was in the hospital for two days with drips coming out of my hands and arms. I remember they gave me Valium to help with detoxing. Mark said he brought the children to see me, and they wept.

Two days later, Mark took me to rehab. He literally threw me on the floor and threw my bags on top of me. He said to the staff something like, "You can have her, I don't want her back."

When I entered rehab, I was sober but remained in a blackout for two weeks. I looked sixty-five years old. My coordination was so bad I could not walk through a doorway. My peripheral vision was not able to see the opening and I would slam my whole body against the wall.

I looked like a victim of domestic violence with my massive black eye. I was not able to put two thoughts together. The staff said I had wet brain and I would never come out of it. I appeared mentally deranged, and the other residents ran away from me because I was so frightening.

The staff said I was the worst case they had ever seen. Now, that is quite a statement for a drug and alcohol rehabilitation center.

Every day was a frightening experience. Sharing a bedroom with a complete stranger made me even more uncomfortable. We all had chores to do, and mine was in the kitchen. There were probably close to eighty women residing there at this present time. We had to go to classes all day long, learning about addiction, relapse, and other subjects pertaining to helping us live drug-free in the outside world.

After two weeks, I gained some clarity and went to church with a couple of other women. I cried out to God, "Look at me! I am physically, emotionally, and spiritually bankrupt! I have been a good servant to you. How could this have happened to me?"

The message from the pastor that day was, "God loves you when you are at your weakest, so he can fill your heart the most."

I got it! My self-will was so strong, I had to be taken to the brink of death so I would finally completely surrender. Once I did that, I was done drinking.

I cried out to God, "Thank you God for saving a wretch like me, but did I really need to go through that much pain?"

The answer was simply, "Yes!"

I knew what lay ahead of me. The physical torture of continuing to detox and the emotional obsession of the monkey mind. This would take time, and as they say in the program, "One day at a time;" but in my case, one hour at a time. Sometimes one minute at a time.

This time around in rehab was insane. Everybody was trying to sneak things in left, right, and center; and believe me, drug addicts and alcoholics are the most dishonest, manipulative, and most dangerous people when they are in their disease. They say an alcoholic will steal your wallet, but an addict will steal your wallet and help you look for it.

When I went into rehab, they gave me a big sister. The one they appointed to me was awesome. She was always available to talk to me anytime of the day or night. She always got on her knees as soon as she got out of bed in the morning. She appeared to have a perfect program down. Please remember this: when someone appears to be too perfect on the outside, they are wearing a mask. We are all human with imperfections. Today, after years of work, I say I am perfectly imperfect.

My roommate was starting to act very strange. At night, she would stutter and walk funny. I thought it was because of the strong sleeping aid she was taking.

On the weekend, all the women would sit and watch a movie in the evening. Well, one night, I had the shock of my life. A counselor walked into my bedroom and came out with a big bottle of vodka. I was speechless. My roommate had been drinking right under my nose. I was so naïve! I thought people came into rehab to get better.

They escorted my roommate out of the bedroom and put her into another room all by herself. The counselor asked me to help search my bedroom. I found four bottles of vodka. They were hidden very well. I asked her, "Don't you want to look through my things?"

She replied, "Of course not."

I didn't understand why she would say that. Just as she was leaving the bedroom, she turned around and noticed a pair of cowboy boots. She said, "Look in those boots will you?"

I went over to the boots and inside was a bottle of vodka. For one split second, I thought to myself, *I am not going to tell her.* I was only about ten days sober and still extremely emotionally unbalanced. However, the fear of it staying there was greater than the fear of drinking it. So I immediately shouted, "Yes, here is another bottle." And I handed it to her.

I started helping the other women in the program as best I could. I got a little sister called Becky. She was very insecure and could not stop obsessing about using. Many years ago, she had gone out to dinner with her parents and witnessed her mother choke to death at the table. Sometimes it is so hard to understand why certain things happen to us in life. They just don't seem fair.

The days in rehab were long and boring. My obsessive thinking remained my constant companion. I was always so tired. We had to get up at 6:00 a.m. every morning, and the staff kept us going all day long. There was no peace due to the chaotic energy of the women. I had to be constantly watching my back. If you accidentally left a personal belonging out, it was gone.

At one point, someone brought in drugs, including heroin, and that was when the staff said enough is enough. They searched all our rooms. Every dresser drawer was emptied, all beds were stripped, and nothing was left unturned. How sad; the staff were trying so hard to help us, and at every turn, some woman simply spoiled it for the rest of us.

On certain Friday nights, we were allowed to go to outside twelve-step meetings. I remember saying at one particular meeting, "I need help!" One kind soul said she would come to see me in rehab and be my temporary sponsor. I really appreciated everything she did for me.

During my stay, I went to church every Sunday. I never missed. The message from the pastor was always something I needed to hear for that week. Eventually, they allowed me to go all by myself.

There were so many gut-wrenching things that happened during my two-month-stay in the center. At one point, our family dog died. It had eaten some poison from the neighbor's yard. Sarah kept telling her father to take the dog to the vet. He never listened until it was too late.

I was allowed to go home for the burial. It was horrible. I could not stop crying. We buried the dog on our property, and I remember the children's eyes. It was an awful experience for everyone. It was even harder driving back to rehab. It was hard concentrating on the road with tears streaming down my face.

Whenever anyone left the center and returned, they always drug-tested the person and physically searched the person and their personal belongings, but they never did that to me. I was always shown favor when I returned and when I walked through the front door, they simply said go to your room.

The next event that only God himself could have orchestrated was when the family moved from the rental house to their newly built home. Mark said, "If you don't come and move all your clothes and personal things from the rental to the new house, I am throwing them in the trash."

I had befriended a young girl in rehab named Stephanie. She was badass and had been on the streets carrying guns and stealing from people's homes. I decided I wanted her to help me accomplish the task. She was only nine days sober, and the staff told me that will never happen. I made an appointment to see the director who ran the rehab and told her what I wanted. She asked if there was anyone else I would consider taking. I told her no, it would take a very strong person to "hold it together" while we moved my things. I wanted Stephanie, and the director allowed her to leave with me for thirteen hours. Not only that, she allowed me to drive her in my personal car to do the job. That was simply against the rules because of insurance purposes. The staff who were on duty that day simply scratched their heads. There are no mistakes in God's world, only divine interventions.

We arrived at the rental house around 9:00 a.m. and started packing my things. Mark always made everything so much more emotionally damaging for the children. He wanted them to take sides and simply forget about me as their mother. It was so obvious he didn't care about anyone except himself. He wanted me to pay at all costs for no longer wanting him as a husband. God knew the real person I was married to, and I simply deserved better. He had the audacity to give me the CDs by Laura Schlinger, *How to Take the Proper Care of a Husband*. He was delusional and simply stated he was the best husband in the world and any woman would be more than happy to have him as her husband. After my awakening, not this woman.

It took Stephanie and myself hours to pack all my things up and move them to the house, but we did with God's powerful presence.

At the end, Stephanie said "That was too hard. Do you want to drink?"

I said, "Absolutely not." The staff had trusted us to go and come back sober, and absolutely nothing was going to stop that from happening, even though I was dying inside from extreme anxiety.

I stopped at Safeway on the way back and bought daffodils for everyone who had helped me that day.

They drug-tested us when we got back. I was clean, but Stephanie was dirty. There was no way she could have used. I had been watching her like a hawk all day long. I made an appointment to see the director and pleaded my case. She believed me. She said we would either be both clean or both dirty, not one clean and one dirty. I thanked her for entrusting me to complete the move sober.

One thing I have learned about myself is when my back is against the wall, I come out fighting. I should say when I feel powerless over a situation, God loads me up with ammunition enough to blow up a small fortress. People have told me my whole life if I put my mind to it, I could achieve anything. However, hopefully, after reading this book, there will be no doubt in your mind that God did for me what I couldn't do for myself. Furthermore, my friend, that is exactly what he can do for you, if you trust him and take the necessary action. God cannot produce miracles in your life without you doing your part.

With God's healing power I was able to transform Stephanie's life. She literally had a spontaneous spiritual experience. She was ready to hear the message from God through me and was now willing to do the work it took to become the woman she was divinely meant to be. Unfortunately, that did not happen for Becky. She was not ready to completely surrender.

The next significant thing that happened was my graduation from the program. It involved three people reading me a poem and giving me a personal message. It also involved passing a glass marble around the room. The significance of the marble was something to the affect that you would throw it when life got too hard.

Now I am going to take you on a brief side-note and then get back to my graduation.

During my stay, there was a woman admitted that had been homeless, living on the streets for quite a few years. She had a hunched back. It was hard to tell if she was a man or a woman. Her clothes were dirty and tattered. The most frightening thing about her was her eyes. I saw complete terror in them. She looked like she had been severely abused and had got to the point where she trusted no one. She would sit outside the building and chain smoke every chance she got. One thing I couldn't believe was someone stole her glasses. Some of those woman who were in rehab behaved like wild animals. She said the homeless people treated her better than the people here. She was right; how sad.

So back to my graduation. The lady I have just been talking about was one of the women who read me a poem and gave me a personal message. Now never ever judge a book by its cover, you may miss the gift. When the marble was passed to her, she held it in her hand while she read the poem. Then afterward, she came really close to me and said, "Anne, look inside the marble, do you see the door?"

I said, "Yes, I do."

She then said, "All you have to do is open it, walk through it to the other side, and you will have a life you could only have dreamt of."

Wow, I was mesmerized and full of hope. Do you know how many times I have remembered those words? Hundreds of times. She changed my life forever.

There is a famous painting of Jesus standing behind a door waiting for a person to open the door and come in. That is the picture I get in my mind when I think of opening the door and walking through it. Accepting Jesus into your life literally changes a person's life forever. Now I told you this was not a religious book. I am not asking you to accept my faith if you don't want to. However, please respect my beliefs, my divine path, and how I listen and follow God's direction always.

I am almost halfway through this book. Now this seems like an odd place in between a chapter to get on my soap box, so here goes.

I don't care if you are Christian, agnostic, atheist, Buddhist, Jewish, Muslim, or whatever you believe in. I don't care what the color of your skin is—you can be white, black, or polka dotted. I don't care if you are rich, middle-class, or poor. I don't care if you are heterosexual, bisexual, or homosexual. I don't care if you are young, middle-aged, or old. I don't care if you are incarcerated, on probation, or walking around a free man. I don't care if you are able-bodied or handicapped. I don't care if you are a learned scholar or you cannot read at all.

What I do care about is that you apply the teachings and use the tools I have laid down in this book to become the amazing person you are meant to be. That you discover your unique gifts and that you are willing to give back to others in order to build a new world. A world where love, peace, communication, productivity, and community are at the center. That we can change our value system from power, control, greed, and fear to love, enlightenment, empowerment, and faith in humanity. That we no longer pollute the earth and show respect to Mother Earth.

The president of the United States doesn't make this country great; it is the people who make America great.

Are you with me? Will you stand by me? Can I count on your support to make this world a better place? Are you willing to take responsibility for your life and do your part? A world where our great grandchildren have a place to live? A world where one brother lifts up another brother? Where one sister extends their hand to another, regardless of race, denomination, or social status? Are you with me? United we stand, divided we fall. The world as we know it will not survive; it will completely die if everyone doesn't do their part.

If you like this book so far, you haven't seen anything yet. This is just the beginning of living my new life. You too can transform your life and experience self-love, integrity, and courage. I believe in you! I believe if you can dream it, you can create it. Every seed that's planted and given empowering energy will germinate and grow. Let's finally stop existing and really start living.

Well, now I got that off my chest, where was I? Oh yes, I was graduating from rehab. Well, Mark decided I was not coming home and that he was divorcing me. He said if I got a lawyer, he would make sure I just had the clothes on my back, never see my children again, and he would trash all my personal things. You see how scary this was? Who in the world is this guy? I couldn't have spent the last twenty-one years with such evil; but alas, I did.

Unfortunately, there are millions of women in emotionally abusive marriages, and there are millions of men like Mark. That is one of the reasons I am writing this book—to help empower people, especially women. One thing I absolutely detest is men who take advantage of women, and vice versa, because they can and they know they can get away with it. They are actually not men but broken little boys.

The staff at the rehab looked for a Sober Living accommodation for me. The closest location to where my children lived was in Napa. Unfortunately, they were full at that present time. I was so shaken up with all these changes that were happening, I asked to stay an extra two weeks in the center.

I was able to stay ten weeks in Marin Services for Women in Marin County for the grand total of $100. Thank goodness Mark had good medical insurance or else I may not have been able to go. Finally, he did something good.

By the time I was ready to leave, a place had become available at the Sober Living in Napa. Before I left, the most amazing thing happened. Becky and some of the women had decided on the last Sunday of my stay to make me a special breakfast. They put a white table cloth on the table. There were special utensils for me to eat with and a fancy water glass. Becky cooked sausage, bacon, eggs, and toast for the occasion. What a feast! So much more delicious than what we normally had to eat.

The happiest moment was when I was given a handmade card with personal testimonies from the women saying how I had helped them and, with God's help, changed the course of their lives.

The front of the card had a rose on it with the inscription "To Anne, Courageous and Full of Spirit." Everyone hugged me and wished me well.

The next day, I left the rehab and I will never forget what the staff told me. They said, "Anne, God saved your life because he has a very special service for you that only you can accomplish. We have never seen anyone go from death to being so alive. Hang on to your sobriety. It is truly a divine gift."

I remember the moment very clearly. I walked out of the main door of the building with my luggage in hand. I fearfully thought to myself, *How is life going to be living sober?*

God, please help me stay sober, one day at a time!

CHAPTER 11

Where Can I Lay My Pillow?

At this point of my journey, I was emotionally unbalanced, fearful, mentally ill, and had no coping mechanisms to deal with life. The one constant I did have was a loving God. I trusted He would put people and create circumstances in my life that would enable me to live happy, joyous, and free. My part was I needed to stay awake and recognize the opportunities that crossed my path and take the necessary action.

Now if you can relate to being at a place in your life where you feel hopeless and helpless, like I was at this stage of my life, I am going to tell you step by step how I transformed into the woman I am today.

So let's take this journey together, and imagine I am holding your hand because we are all brothers and sisters. We are all connected so allow my journey to be the catalyst for your transformation. Are you willing to do the work necessary to become the best version of yourself? I want you to deliberately make that decision right now. Are you committed or not? All you need is the faith the size of a mustard seed to move mountains. When you honestly make a decision to become a new you, the energy goes into the universe and starts a chain reaction.

Say right now, out loud, "I am committed to do the work necessary to become the best version of myself. I deserve a life full of love, abundance, and joy. I am willing to let go of the past, and I claim my right to be free, to be me."

I did not hear you! Say it again and again until it is embedded into your subconscious and believe you play a very important part in transforming this world. If you contribute in a small or big way, it doesn't matter. It matters that you take action. My life purpose is no more important than yours. The reason God chose me for my purpose is because I am a warrior. I am courageous, tenacious, and his voice can be heard through me. Believe me, I did not step up willingly for this service, but because of what God has done for me in my life, I want to tell the world.

If writing this book and telling you about my life journey can help you or anyone in any way to lessen your suffering, give you self-awareness, and give you courage to take the first step to living a new way of life, I have accomplished my life purpose.

So, my friends, stay open, be present, be courageous, and most of all, know you are unique and powerful. The world is waiting for you to do your best, to become your best, and know you are the best version of you.

I left Marin Services for Women in April 2006. I drove to the Sober Living accommodation in Napa. I paid for my first month's rent and was greeted by the manager running the house where I would be living. I was escorted to my room and I started unpacking my things. I was so full of anxiety. I could feel my heart beating through my shirt and I felt alone and frightened. Who would I be sharing a room with? She would be a perfect stranger. Would she be nice or mean?

There were four more women living in the house. They all looked very uncomfortable in their own skin. I really didn't want to be here, but I had nowhere else to go. I longed for my pillow, my comfortable bed, and all the comforts of home.

The first night, the manager was supposed to help me adjust to living on the outside. It is quite terrifying the first few days for anyone leaving rehab and trying to adjust to new surroundings. I knocked on her bedroom door that evening only to find her stumbling all over the place and completely out of it. I thought she was drunk. I immediately called the owner and he tried to ease my fears but my body was already in the fight, flight, and freeze state. I wanted to run, but again, I asked myself, "Where am I going to run to?"

All the other women were in their rooms with the TV on and my roommate had gone away for a couple of days.

I eventually went to sleep, and the next day, one of the woman said she would take me to a twelve-step meeting.

In the past, I didn't want to ask for help. I had severe trust and abandonment issues. All my so-called family members had emotionally abused me, so why would I ask for help from a stranger? However, that is the first step that one needs to take. The admission I am powerless over alcohol and my life has become unmanageable. All twelve-step programs are "we" programs, not "I" programs. So I knew I needed to ask for a sponsor.

Every habit has three stages. The trigger, the routine, and the reward. First step is to recognize you have a problem and ask for help. I announced at the meeting I had just left rehab and needed a sponsor. Someone stepped up and said she would work with me.

I did not like living in Sober Living; however, one of the women was very kind to me and took me under her wing. I simply had to take one day at a time or fear would take over me and I would become paralyzed.

Take one day at a time.

I went to a lot of meetings and started working the twelve-step program with my sponsor. It was a full-time job staying sober, and I just didn't need the added pressure of being served with divorce papers and the start of endless court hearings. Furthermore, Mark told me I needed to move all my things out of the house or they were going into the trash.

I asked one of the guys that was living in the men's Sober house to help me move my things. He was an absolute Godsend. I hired a moving truck and we went one weekend over to the house to collect all my things. At that time, I was so fearful of Mark. Just the mention of his name, let alone his voice, put me in a state of terror. He was a big bully and loved causing emotional pain to me and anyone else who he believed crossed him.

I thought I was going to lose it, but the guy helping me to move was simply amazing. He comforted me and told me to stay calm and focus. When he walked into the house, he confidently walked up to

Mark, shook his hand, and introduced himself. We both had very little sobriety, but God empowered us to fulfill the task at hand. I rented a storage unit and we moved all my things into it.

Now I don't know if you have thought to yourself, where did she get the money? Well, when I turned in my Fidelity funds, I got around $6,000. Without that money, I would have been completely stranded. God knew the path I would have to take, and that is why that event had to happen. Wow, doesn't that just take your breath away? God was already making sure I had some funds for the future back in 2005.

I had been in Sober Living for about a month now. I was attending a lot of meetings and I would carry a small notebook around with me and write down what I considered "the gold" from the meeting. The gold being snips of information I could read over and over again to give me hope on my journey in sobriety. One of the most important things I heard was, "Always look up to the sunlight of the spirit."

Have faith in a power greater than yourself. A power that will guide you, protect you, and love you no matter what.

It is almost impossible to feel that presence when your body is a bundle of nerves. However, be rest assured your higher power of your own understanding is omnipresent.

One of the meetings I attended was just around the corner, and I would go there frequently. One evening, a new man appeared, and after the meeting, he wanted to talk to me. He told me he had just arrived here from Germany. He stated he had multiple sclerosis and had arrived in a wheelchair but, because of the power of prayer, was able to walk again. He asked me about my story, and during our talk, my intuition told me there was something wrong with him. I couldn't tell you what it was, but a red flag went up. After our conversation, I wasn't interested in talking to him again.

Your body is very in tune with energies. Don't ignore the signals it is trying to tell you. If your body starts feeling nervous, it is saying, "Warning! Warning! Back away!"

Me and the other women in the program had been warned against the men in the program taking advantage of newcomers. They called it thirteenth stepping.

The next week, I attended a meeting at a building called Sea Scouts. There were over sixty people there, including the man I had just talked about. After the meeting, I met outside with my sponsor. The odd man stood close to us. My sponsor said, turning to the man, "You can trust him, he is safe."

"What?" I said alarmingly. "Trust him?"

"Yes," replied my sponsor.

I couldn't believe my ears. The man, named Thomas, was grinning from ear to ear.

Well, at this point, I needed as many supportive members from the twelve-step group to help me on my journey. I exchanged telephone numbers with Thomas and he said he would be in touch with me very soon.

He called me the next day and invited me to dinner. As we were talking at the dinner table, he suddenly remarked, "You're sane."

I said, "Well, I always thought I was, but my parents and Mark didn't think so!"

I told him how unstable I was with all the stress around the divorce and being early in sobriety. He had twenty years sobriety but went out and now had around four years. When I asked him why he went out drinking again, he said he had kept a secret and not told his sponsor.

Drinking is but a symptom of the real problem. We are only as sick as our secrets. Be honest and share everything with another person; it takes the power out of it.

He said he was going to share all the knowledge he had learned in recovery over the last thirty years with me. He was going to give me a crash course. Thomas and the lady that took me under her wing in the Sober Living house said they could not believe how quickly my mind could pick up information and apply it to my life.

Listen carefully to other people's life experiences and learn. It may save you a lot of heartache, pain, and precious time.

At this stage of my recovery, life was hard. The Sober Living house was not run well, so I didn't feel any sense of stability and security. I was going through the divorce court, and my attorney was getting absolutely nowhere. In fact, I am going to keep this part of my story somewhat short and not spare you all the details.

I had not really seen the children because I was emotionally very weak, and to see them would mean driving to Mark's house to pick them up. I simply could not stand to see him. His face in court was one of a man who was determined to give me nothing. He looked angry and vindictive.

Thomas was an amazing distraction. He would make me laugh until I literally peed my pants. He was very interesting to talk to; some said he was a genius. He said I was the only person he had known that had a brain that could keep up with his.

Laughter is the best form of medicine to relieve stress. Laugh every day.

I had been working the steps with my sponsor, but unfortunately, she did not believe in God, so we were not a good match. I started working the steps with Thomas. He was extremely knowledgeable about the twelve steps. He said over the span of thirty years, 500 people had approached him about working the steps with him. Only twelve people had completed all the steps, and he said I was the most willing of them all. I was extremely unusual in that I was so willing to do the work necessary to complete the steps quickly and conscientiously. I wanted desperately to get some freedom from my monkey mind and gain some tools to use in my life.

The greater your physical, emotional, and spiritual bottom, the greater your willingness to do the work necessary to grow.

Back to life in Sober Living. The manager running the house wanted everyone to kiss her ass. I got falsely accused of doing something, and she wanted me to apologize. No way was I going to do that. I don't kiss anybody's ass. I packed my things and, knowing I had nowhere to go, put my faith in God that he would provide.

One of the neighbors said she would let me stay with her for a couple of days. I moved all my things into her house only to come home a day later to find her totally wasted. Her secret was exposed, so she asked me to leave.

Having nowhere to go, I had to book into a motel. Thomas was there every step of the way, helping me pack and unpack. I was in a very difficult situation. I could not rent an apartment because I had no income to show to meet the requirements.

You have to have documented proof when submitting an application to a property management company that you are making three times the monthly rent.

I secured a temporary job as a caregiver, but as soon as I moved my things in, I was forced to move my things out. What a hopeless mess I was in. I moved back into the motel. I knew my money was running out and could not stay there for long.

Now about Thomas. I will never be able to explain who or what he was. His demeanor and physical appearance would literally change before my eyes depending on his mood. Most people would have gone screaming and running down the street as far away from him as possible. Not me. He got my curiosity; *how in the world did he do that?* I was convinced I was going to find out. It was like watching a scary movie, except I was one of the leading characters.

I have the mind of a detective. I love solving the unexplainable when it involves my interaction with bizarre people. Thomas knew things about me that he could never have known. For example, he knew what my favorite childhood stuffed animal was, a koala bear; that was something I had never told anyone. He also said I had always asked God to put his hands on my shoulders; again, I had never told another soul about that. I always questioned if Thomas was from God or from the devil. However, he always did far more good than harm. He, like most of us, wanted to do good, but the demons inside of him took over when he was triggered.

The motel I stayed in was in Napa. The whole property was surrounded by weeds. Thomas knew I loved flowers, and one morning, when I looked out of my bedroom window, there were flowers everywhere. I told him, "You did this, didn't you?"

He just grinned from ear to ear. One morning, he asked me if I wanted him to go to Pete's Coffee and get me a mocha. I said, "That would be great, thank you!" He left the bedroom, closed the door, and one minute later, knocked on the door and was standing there with a mocha from Pete's. There was no way he could have driven there and back from the coffee shop in that time.

Who was Thomas? Where exactly did he come from? Another man in the recovery program had grown up with him and gave me some background information. He just said Thomas was a genius but had been badly abused as a child. Because of the abuse, he had developed multiple personalities.

Thomas worked all twelve steps of the recovery program with me. I was so excited and willing to do the work in order to gain some emotional freedom. One of the biggest "aha" moments was I had given away my power to other people. I had let my parents and Mark define who I was. That I was stupid, unlovable, and would never be able to take care of myself. They said those things in order to control me. They wanted to take a hostage. It was not true. I am intelligent, lovable, and when push comes to shove, I can take care of myself. I got on a plane and came to America all by myself, didn't I? When someone describes you in a negative way, what kind of distorted filters are they looking through. Usually if someone has done absolutely no work on themselves, their filters are not allowing them to see the truth. They live in denial. Their ego has created a false self because it is too painful to live in the real world and face the truth.

Don't give your power away to other people who don't really know you. People who themselves are living in denial live chaotic lives and bare no fruit as a result of their toil. Go seek advice from an experienced counsellor, sponsor, or someone who is spiritually fit.

Thomas knew of someone who was living in an apartment complex and was going to be leaving shortly. He asked them to put in a good word for me at the property management office. We devised a plan that my parents would write a letter saying I had a trust fund and that is where I would get the money to support myself.

In the meantime, Thomas described, to a tee, a house that one of my friends lived in. I had not spoken to them in years. Thomas encouraged me to call them and ask them if I could stay with them until the apartment was available and I got a letter from my parents.

My friends allowed me to stay with them in the interim. How in the world did Thomas know all these things?

I eventually moved into the apartment with virtually no money. However, when I was down to my last $200, I got part of a settlement from the divorce proceedings that put me in a good financial position.

I eventually had a place, a bedroom, and a bed to finally lay my pillow on. I was simply exhausted from all the moving, but I know I could never have done it without my angel with one broken wing.

CHAPTER 12

To Thine Own Self Be True

I continued working through the twelve step program with Thomas. Working the steps was not hard for me because I was very enthusiastic about gaining some emotional stability. I wanted that spiritual awakening they talked about in step twelve. I also wanted the promises to come true, especially the part where it says we can now handle situations that used to baffle us.

Another piece of evidence that came to light was I wasn't in touch with reality. My ego had created a false self, due to trauma; it was too painful to face the truth. The truth being I was a very sick woman emotionally with no tools to live life on life's terms.

The truth will set you free. The more you can live in the truth, the more emotionally balanced you will become.

One very important factor you need to consider is can you trust your sponsor/counsellor/spiritual adviser completely? If the answer is yes, that is half the battle. If the answer is no, remember to listen to your body, then find someone else.

Take responsibility for your new journey; only you can do the work. Believe in yourself, one step at a time.

Between working the steps and continually laughing my ass off with Thomas, the continual attendance of court hearings was less painful.

The divorce hearings were incomprehensible. Mark lived in a multimillion-dollar home with monthly payments of at least $8,000, and his income tax return showed he made $1,800 a month. I never got what I deserved, and on top of that, Mark had told a friend of mine he had buried his money so deep I would never find it.

> Life is not fair. Learn life's lessons so
> you know how to break them.
> —Dalai Lama.

Another important lesson to learn about people. When someone shows you their true self, believe them. They are not going to change without honest self-awareness and action.

Unfortunately, because the lawyers were getting all the money, Mark and I had to settle out of court, which meant I definitely wasn't going to get a good settlement.

However, I was so grateful to be single and sober. You cannot put a price on that. Always be grateful for the smallest things. Gratitude makes you feel happy, reduces stress, gives you more resilience, and makes you sleep better. *Always have an attitude of gratitude.*

Talking about gratitude, at six months sober, I started going into the women's jail in Napa. Me and another woman would run a recovery meeting once a month in the jail. The women were very grateful to hear our experiences, strength, and hope. I continued doing that for the next eight years until the Napa earthquake.

You certainly don't have to be in recovery to help others. You can share your story with all kinds of people. Women who have children the same age as yours. Women who are on welfare. People who are homeless. People who divinely cross your path. It could be someone in the supermarket, at a local park, in a department store. Someone who needs a smile, a door opened, a bag carried, a genuine hug to know someone cares. You will be amazed what a single kind gesture can do for another human being.

Pass it forward. Show love in all the dark places. Help illuminate another person's soul. Think of others besides yourself. The homeless person on the corner of the street wasn't always homeless. They started out just like you.

What is very interesting about my journey is everything I wasn't given in life from my loved ones I now gave to others. I was never given unconditional love, compassion, joy, and a stable and secure environment. I give these things to everyone around me. God has been my constant teacher. He is my father, friend, constant companion, confidant, and spiritual adviser to name a few.

He showed me how to love by loving me. He showed me compassion so I could show compassion to others. He gave me a joyful heart because I had the assurance He will never let me down. He forgave me of my sins through Jesus Christ who died on the cross for all our sins.

It is the Saint Francis of Assisi prayer. Give and you will receive. Give unto others as you would want others to give to you.

An interesting twist to why Mark eventually divorced me (he actually never wanted to). This is a man who doesn't believe in the power of God or the spirit world. He said when I was in rehab, something came to him in the middle of the night and told him he must release me. I guess an angel or maybe Jesus himself came to deliver the message. I am so glad that happened. I could never have been happily married to Mark ever again.

God wants you to have the desires of your heart. Listen to his direction and take the necessary action. Remember, you don't have to do anything alone.

To do the fifth step of the twelve step program, it involves admitting to God and to another human being the exact nature of your wrongs. Thomas decided we should go away for a couple of days and undertake this process in different surroundings. He decided we would go to Las Vegas. He said he was not going to gamble.

If you have never been to Las Vegas, it is a wonderful place to go. There are all kinds of things to do besides drinking and gambling. So we packed our bags and off we went.

We did the fifth step of my recovery program the day after we got there. I didn't feel this tremendous release people talk about, but I did feel some sense of relief. Unfortunately after that, Thomas decided to go gambling. As he lost more and more money, he turned into an angry monster. When we got back to the bedroom, he started throwing chairs around. I was terrified, but I had nowhere to go.

We did get home sober and in one piece, thank goodness. After we had completed the rest of the steps, I prayed to God and said, "Get him out of my life. He is dangerous."

I don't really understand the particulars, all I know is he got on a plane and went back to Germany. However, he did say one thing: "God must really love you. He sent me here from Germany to help you. Now my work is done. I am going back." He told me I restored his faith in humanity. He said I loved him unconditionally, even though he was emotionally broken, and I was his greatest teacher. Actually, it was God working through me that was his greatest teacher.

I had enormous compassion for Thomas. He had been tortured as a child physically, emotionally, and mentally. No one deserves to be treated that way; how cruel and self-centered parents and siblings can be! When people don't have God in their lives, they resort to their primitive ways and act like vicious animals.

With all the violence, fear, and the breakdown of society today, people shout out to God, "Please help us."

God whispers, "I will, when you listen."

I want to ask you a question right now. What would it take for you to step out of your comfort zone today? What conditions need to be put in place? Can you walk your talk?

There is never a perfect time nor a perfect set of conditions when it is time to take action. The right time is *now*, today, in this moment.

You picked up this book to read for a reason. You are motivated to become the best version of yourself. I hope, up to now, I have inspired you to take the first step. Let's continue with my story.

Thomas had now left for Germany, and I felt sad and lonely. I missed the laughter. However, it simply wasn't safe being around Thomas when he was angry. Some people can actually go into blackouts when they rage and totally become unconscious of their actions.

One of the men in the program asked astonishingly how I got away from Thomas. He said he was a con man, and the other women that he had been involved with got drunk. He said I must be spiritually fit. Well, after dealing with Mark, I had become an expert on the working mind of a sociopath. I had learned all their tricks and moves to try and control me. All I can say is this: without Thomas's help, I don't know if I would have stayed sober with all the pressures of the divorce and all the moving I had to do. Thank you, God, for sending me a helper. *When you are spiritually fit, you can do anything.*

I am now about nineteen months sober. I was able to complete all twelve steps with Thomas before he left for Germany. The steps involved making amends with the people we harmed when we were drinking. I loved this step; making amends with my children was so important.

What I love about step work is you learn about your character defects and how they affected others. I changed my whole approach to parenting after working step five. I don't try and control my children anymore. I treat them like adults. I let them learn from their own mistakes. I give advice only when they ask for it. Our children are not ours to own. They are individuals lent to us for safekeeping for a short while. They must forge their own path in life.

However, when children are young, it is important to actively and consciously implant a positive, encouraging, and healthy foundation. I told Sarah from an early age, "If I could pick any daughter in the whole world, it would be you!" I constantly told her that for years. However, the conversation, after a year, went something like this: "If I could pick any daughter in the whole world—"

"It would be me, it would be me," and she would have a smile from ear to ear.

Sarah has great self-esteem and tells me she is awesome. I think it made a difference telling her I would pick her out of all the daughters in the world to be mine. She completed a four-year college degree by the age of twenty-one and is now in graduate school.

It is also important to set healthy boundaries and discipline your children. They want structure. Now that is where I fell short. I remember threatening them with restrictions and trying to set boundaries. A typical response from my son was, "Stop saying those things, Mom, you are not going to do anything to us. You love us too much." Oh boy, some kids are just too smart.

Yes, I delighted in my children, even though they were stubborn and willful. Must have taken after their father; could not have been me, do you think?

By the time my children were thirteen and ten, I had video-taped one hundred hours of their lives. They sometimes complained at the time but love watching the videos now. I didn't want to miss anything and thought, *When I am old, I can sit in my rocking chair and watch them.*

My children responded, "You, old? never!"

This chapter and the following chapters are devoted to sharing with you all the knowledge, wisdom, enlightening, and empowering tools I have learned and applied to my life. However, I want to mention a few things that can get in the way of starting something new.

Firstly, you will be so excited with the thought of doing something different, but when you try and start the new task at hand, you will get push back. Your ego will give you a list of excuses why you cannot start today.

I had been told by quite a few people over the years that I needed to write a book about my life, but I was only in love with the idea. The first excuse I came up with was I didn't want to write this book while my parents were alive. I believe in always honoring my parents. However, in order for you to fully understand why I was so handi-capped, living life on life's terms, I had to explain what happened to me as a child. One of the hardest things for me to understand was what made my parents the way they are. My mother refused to tell me anything about her childhood, so what made her so non-empa-thetic and unloving? What made my father so fearful?

When I was young and we went to the store, every window was closed and locked down with a special key. There were two doors you would have to open, close, and lock both at the front and back entrance to the house before existing. Every electrical cord attached to an appliance had to be unplugged from the wall or else the whole house would burn down when we were at the store. That is the behavior of someone paralyzed with fear.

Part of forgiving another person is understanding where they came from and what happened to them on their journey. The English are well-known for having a stiff upper lip and, at any cost, don't want to air their "dirty laundry" to the world.

The second excuse I came up with was I said to God, what can I possibly say and do that hasn't already been said and done. There are thousands of authors, speakers, and workshops that address the process of transformation. I don't have anything new to contribute. Let's be realistic here. I am not delusional about how hard it is for people to step out of their comfort zone.

The third excuse, and probably the most applicable, was since my divorce, I had been living in noisy apartment buildings. Where I presently live, my next door neighbor is extremely self-centered. She doesn't care what kind of disturbance she causes me and other tenants. I told God, "I cannot write a book here. I would not be able to concentrate. I will write the book when I move somewhere quiet and more conducive with the environment for writing."

The fourth excuse was I simply didn't want the responsibility that goes along with writing my biography and stepping into my purpose.

Well, there you are; aren't those valid excuses? You would agree with me, right? I don't need to write this book. Not!

I will explain further in the book how these excuses held no water. But first let me wallow in my pity party (I have a big grin on my face). We have all been there, done that!

Now let's put all our excuses behind us and start an amazing journey together. I am really excited to be given this opportunity to share my experience, strength, and hope with you. I hope you will honestly believe you are destined to becoming the amazing person you were divinely meant to be.

We are like the slab of marble Michael Angelo worked on. He just chipped away all the unwanted material to reveal the masterpiece that lay within. Now let us do the same. I cannot wait to see your true masterpiece!

CHAPTER 13

I Give You Permission

Regarding the first excuse about my parents. My father is nine-ty-two years old, and my mother ninety. I have no idea how long they will live and don't want to know. I just want to love them each and every day. God is in charge of how long they will live; that's all I need to know. God always takes care of the details perfectly. God has always reminded me of the urgency to write this book, regardless if my parents are still alive.

Regarding the second excuse, "God, what am I going to say that has not already been said?"

During quiet time with God, He told me He was going to take me into the future. He was going to show me how the earth would look 150 years from now, the struggles mankind would have to deal with in the future if there was no shift in consciousness, and if man did not turn to him.

Well, I consider myself very open to God's messages that He gives to me. However, in this case, I have to admit I was excited and somewhat hesitant about telling anyone about this.

I signed up at the beginning of this year to take a workshop on quantum power. The teacher confirmed my thoughts on how the spiritual world works. However, she stated in the space created with quantum power, you could go to the future and bring information back to today. I almost fell off my chair. Was I hearing her right? This was definite confirmation from the outside work that what God had told me was correct.

The teacher had given me permission to explore this with an open mind. If my ego started telling me this was not possible, I could easily ignore it. I had mentioned my vision with three other students taking the course, and they simply ignored the whole conversation I had with each of them at different times. They all pretended like I never said anything. Talk about feeling invisible.

One week later, when I was meditating on emptiness, God gave me a complete download. So my friends, I want to share this with you. Maybe knowing what the future holds will be the catalyst for you taking the first step to becoming the best version of you.

Before God downloaded this information, he gave me an image of Earth. Everywhere you looked was dry, humid, and dark. It looked like a desert. No plant life, no trees, mother nature no longer existed. Everyone lived in tattered tents. People looked dirty and unkempt.

Message from God to the World with Me Being the Intercessor

If you don't take conscious action, you will die.

If you don't love your neighbor, he will rise up and strike you down.

If you don't keep the commandments, you have no rules to live by.

Your children will be cursed with mental illness.

Your children will not love you.

Your body will be plagued with illness.

Each day will seem like eternal darkness.

No light or energy will emerge from you or mother Earth.

You will live in a constant state of survival.

You will trust no one.

You will live with shame and guilt.

People will steal from you.

Violence will be an everyday occurrence.

Crops will not grow because the soil is infertile. Food will be scarce. No natural resources.

Children will die young. Elderly left to die.

The world is as healthy and strong as the weakest person.

Darkness will cover the light, and your mind will become dull.

You will never see a rainbow again because of the pollution in the air.

Humans are frail and self-destructive without Me.

Even the rich will not escape.

Satanic gods will try and rule the world.

All this will happen if you do not listen to Me and follow my direction.

Humble yourselves or your pride will destroy you.

You must consciously and wholeheartedly choose Me (God).

Seek the goodness within and water it daily.

Step out of your comfort zone and take responsibility for your life.

Being selfish is the coward's way out.

Christians should be spiritual warriors.

Believing in Me gives people strength, courage, and endurance.

If you are one with Me, you are love, and love conquers all; there is no substitute.

Be honest always and seek the truth.

You have run out of excuses. Your choice is to live or die.

Visualize a new world.

So let all this information settle in your mind. Really digest the magnitude of the situation. Don't let your mind tell you this will not happen.

This is true reality.

Meditate on this situation. Go within and listen carefully. What does your inner voice say? What does your body tell you? Do you have any sense of knowing the truth from lies? Write the messages down on a piece of paper so you don't forget. It is amazing how much intuition and discernment we have over situations if we just sit still for fifteen minutes or more and listen. Remember, the power of now.

In this moment in time, if we can be present, there is no fear. With no fear present, the mind can be clear and have freedom to see what is true reality. We are able to be true to ourselves.

The third excuse was I cannot write a book living in apartments; it was simply too noisy. Especially living next to my present neighbor who cares nothing about how her actions affect others. She has a constantly barking dog, she smokes, and our balconies are connecting. But the worst thing is her boyfriend slamming the front door which shakes the whole apartment building. He doesn't work, so he was doing this all day long. The noise had brought on my post-traumatic stress. When the door slammed, I would go into the fight, flight, or freeze state. I had become a complete nervous wreck. The noise of the door slamming represented anger to me. I then developed fibromyalgia in my neck and shoulders and wasn't able to lift either of my arms. The pain was so excruciating, I could do nothing.

I was so angry that management would never take care of any complaints I reported, so I wrote a three-page complaint letter addressed to the owner of the apartment complex. My sponsor and my friend said not to send the letter. So I said to God I need a sign regarding whether I should send the letter or not. I thought carefully and said, "God if I see the owner of the property outside in near proximity, around Fairfield, that will be the signal to send it to him." Now the chances of that happening were zero, because he lived one and a half hours away from Fairfield in a ritzy town.

About a week later, it was my son's birthday. I wanted to take him to Mary's Pizza Shack and then a movie. We love going to Mary's for the lasagna. There were three of us that went out to dinner, and there was much laughter and excitement. In fact, I was so excited, I didn't not notice the owner of the senior apartments and his parents sitting behind us. I was flabbergasted to say the least.

After the evening's event, I was so excited to tell my sponsor, but again she discouraged me to send the letter. My friend said the same thing. I was astonished by their answers. I said, "How am I going to receive God's gift if I don't take the necessary action?" So I emailed the letter, and on Monday, the owner knocked on my neighbor's door. He told the boyfriend if he received one more complaint about the door being slammed, he would be evicted, and the owner said a few more choice words. No more slamming doors. My pain subsided within a week.

So I was lying on my bed one afternoon, and all of a sudden, I said to myself, "Well, God took care of the slamming door, and my pain subsided. I had better get up and start writing my book." I had no previous experience with writing, except for a few poems I had written over the years. However, when God asks you to do something, He will equip you with the skills to fulfill the task. He will not allow you to fail. It is obvious who would continue to have faith in Him if He did not carry you through the service He requested of you.

When God asks me to fulfill a service, I never look through my eyes at accomplishing the task. I look through God's eyes. If he asks me to do something, I can do it. I would never have started writing this book if I thought I was doing this alone. I cannot do anything by myself. I can only complete the service at hand with His help.

When I look through my eyes, I see my brokenness. However, when I look through God's eyes at myself, I see a faithful, courageous, compassionate spiritual warrior. He actually makes me feel special, unique, purposeful and, most of all, loved unconditionally. Anne means grace, and God has truly showed me amazing grace. I have tears in my eyes. I will never lose the gratitude I have for God and the life he has provided for me. Mystical, miraculous, and unexplainable events have happened in my life because I trusted, obeyed, and believed all things are possible with God.

All things are possible with God.

The last excuse, I did not want to take responsibility; well, you will have to read the rest of the book to find the answer.

So each subsequent chapter will cover my journey from 2008 to today. It will cover lessons I learned, tools I used, and the mystical experiences I have had with God.

In chapter 26, I will suggest simple steps you can start doing immediately. You will see an almost immediate difference on your outlook to life, how you feel about yourself, and have a clearer vision of what your gift is to the world.

CHAPTER 14

Knock, Knock, Who's There?

I t is now 2008, and I am coming to the end of my divorce. Finally, time to take a deep breath. I am shocked and somewhat resentful how it all ended, but there are no mistakes in God's world.

I was living in my apartment in Napa and suffering from the flu. This is a very rare occurrence. I never get sick other than having bad allergies. I was lying in bed and trying to keep warm when suddenly I heard my doorbell ring. I eventually managed to drag myself out of bed and went to see who it was. There was a bag of food outside. I was amazed. I said to myself, "For me?" I looked around and saw Benjamin walking away from my apartment. He was a guy that I knew from the twelve-step program. He was a man who had a gentle soul, something hard to find in others these days.

I shouted, "Benjamin, Benjamin!"

He finally heard my voice and turned around and came walking back to the apartment. He knew I was sick and had brought me a whole bag of groceries including warm minestrone soup and Vicks to rub on my chest. That was one of the kindest things anybody had ever done for me. He wanted to come into the apartment, but I told him I did not want him to catch my flu. He said he was not concerned about that and proceeded to pick up the bag of groceries and walk into my kitchen. We sat down at the table and had minestrone soup and crackers.

I had this awakening that I simply wasn't used to anybody taking care of me. I had been so self-reliant my whole life. It felt unusual to actually receive care from Benjamin. Now that is a sad statement to actually say out loud. I felt a sense of belonging which was a wonderful new feeling, if only temporary.

I started hiking with Benjamin, and we became really good friends. When I was with him, I felt a sense of comradeship. He was a real gentleman and very kind. He got to meet my children and we all got along amicably.

After I got into sobriety, I went to get a full medical examination, including blood work. Everything was normal, and all my blood results indicated I was in good health. Now this was definitely a miracle. A woman of my physical status, drinking vodka 24/7 for three years should have had at least some abnormal liver results. Now do you believe in miracles? I definitely do and today I anticipate them happening all the time and I am never disappointed.

Our life is not our own.

What do I mean by that? Well, before we came down from heaven, our souls had already decided on their life purpose. However, when we are born, all that memory is erased. But we have already decided on who will be our parents, who will be our spouse, and all other major partnerships throughout our lives. Why? Well, before we can do our life purpose, we have to go through the trials which cause us immense pain, which hopefully leads us on a path to self-discovery. This in turn should teach us our life lessons, which develops our divine gifts, which leads us to help others and then change the world.

Well, there you have it. Unfortunately, if you don't learn the lesson the first time around—and no one does because of our egos—the lesson keeps coming around and around until we finally get it. Along with that, the pain gets stronger and stronger until you finally surrender. It is up to you; the easy way or the hard way? You have a choice.

You always have a choice with everything in life. It is up to you. Pain is inevitable, suffering is optional.

In conclusion, your life is not your own. You path has already been mapped out. How many detours do you want to take? The good news is with age, hopefully, comes wisdom. I am definitely stubborn, but no one can call me stupid. I know a good thing when I see it and hang onto it with both hands. Wisdom brings discernment. Discernment allows you to make good choices. Good choices lead to a joyful, purposeful, and somewhat balanced life. You have a choice.

Do you want to be right or do you want peace?

From a medical point of view, I was extremely healthy. Just for your information, it takes about eighteen months for alcohol to completely leave your body. With drugs, it can take years to become completely clean.

I told my children to be aware of addictions. Once you're hooked to something, it can be impossible to break free.

During my volunteer work in the women's jail, the women would tell me, "It's not my children that come visit me anymore but my grandchildren." That is a true realization. If you never hit rock bottom, you could be in your insidious disease for twenty to thirty years; or worse yet, die in your addiction. Remember, I told you someone dies in the world every three seconds from addiction.

The one thing that was a real problem from the very beginning of my recovery was my lack of sleep. It was virtually impossible for me to sleep through the night. I would wake up several times during the night, and when I got up in a morning, I would immediately want to go back to bed. Most of my days were very unproductive.

My doctor had prescribed several different sleeping aids, but nothing had worked. Being a recovering alcoholic, the doctor had to be very careful not to prescribe a product that could open my neuropathways which would bring on the phenomenon of craving for alcohol. I was tenacious. Every time I visited him, I reminded him I was an alcoholic. Warning, warning. Unfortunately, my fear became my reality. My doctor prescribed something that brought on the craving to drink.

I reacted, screaming and shouting, saying, "This cannot happen! I have worked so hard keeping my sobriety!" I literally was holding onto the kitchen table because I felt like a piece of rope was tied to my foot, dragging me to the liquor store.

Benjamin was there and somewhat concerned and fearful. Sarah was with me for the weekend, and Benjamin was trying to keep her calm and give her reassuring words that everything would be okay.

I woke up at 2:00 a.m. on a Sunday morning and called Benjamin up on the phone. I remember him saying, "You're not going to drink, are you?" At that very moment, I knew the only thing that could save me was God. It says in our literature that there will be a point in our sobriety when no human power can save us from the first drink, only a power greater than ourselves.

I prayed to God, asking him to keep me sober. It took about forty-eight hours for the craving for alcohol to disappear. Wow, that was a close call! Thank you, God, for hearing my cries for help and keeping me sober.

Another interesting event in 2008 was a workshop I attended in Sacramento. It was a three-day event and we stayed in the actual building where the workshop was held. The purpose like all these similar events is more or less the same—uncover the brokenness within and build a new you. I am going to describe some of the exercises I went through. There were six participants. Also, we were not allowed to have contact with anyone while we were there. No cell phones allowed.

There were about five counsellors plus the director of the program. We all had to let the counselors describe who they thought we were. I was called "the stainless steel strawberry." I think you understand the concept. The names were meant to shake us up and reveal the masks we were wearing.

Another very interesting exercise was we were all on a boat and only two could survive. Pick the two people you choose to let live, and we had to look at each of the other people in the eye and tell them, "I choose to let you die." What I found amazing was I was the only one that included myself as one of the survivors. All the rest would have let themselves die and allow two other people to live.

The two people I chose to survive were myself and the only man in the group. What I took away from the exercise was I am a survivor. I have a need to survive no matter what the circumstances. This sense of self-preservation is necessary to get through life. Life is not fair, and bad things sometimes happen to good people. It is necessary to find the courage within to step through the fire and come out of the other side. Of course, the exercise is fictitious, it would never happen. We are not God. We are powerless over all situations.

Courage is not the absence of fear; courage is walking through the fear.

One of the greatest spiritual teachers of our time says life is not here to make us happy, it is here to increase our consciousness; or another way of saying it is becoming more self-aware.

Another exercise was we had to sit in a corner of a room, facing the corner, and proceed to scream at a person we felt had harmed us in the past.

There would be loud music playing in the background. Good exercise. Sometimes we are so angry, we simply cannot put pen to paper or take any sort of action because we are so traumatized by an event.

The last exercise I remember was very interesting. The director gave us two songs that we had to lip-sync to. She was really intuitive and carefully selected the songs that pertained to each of our lives. We were given the songs one evening, and the next day, we would have to perform.

The songs she chose for me were "I Will Survive" by Gloria Gainer and "The Rose" by Bette Midler. One of the women lent me a black sequined dress to wear for the song "I Will Survive." Some of the women stayed up all night practicing. Not me; I wanted my sleep.

The next morning, everyone was so excited about performing. It was very interesting watching how people played out their roles.

I was one of the last ones to perform. I remember wearing the black sequined dress and walked onto the stage like I owned the place. As I lip-synced, I shook my hips, I gyrated up and down as I pretended to point my finger at Mark telling him I would survive. The point was to solidify in my subconscious that I could get through this difficult time in my life.

When it came to singing "The Rose," I remember starting to sing the song and wanting to really express my feelings but felt I would appear overdramatic. In a split second, I said to myself, "Just go for it." I put all these amazing moves to help interpret the meaning of the words of the song.

I had no idea how I looked, but toward the end of the song, I looked over at everyone. All the counsellors, the director, and some of the group were crying their eyes out. I was shocked. At the end of the song, I crouched really low and pretended to be a rose bud slowly growing up from the ground and becoming a beautiful rose. As soon as I stopped, one of the women said, "That could have been on TV. It was so good!" The director said she had never seen anyone perform their songs so good.

So what's my point? Well, when you are purposefully living your life, listening to the spirit, and following your divine path, things will appear. Not only do you learn enlightening and powerful tools to help your journey, find courage to walk through trials, but you start to identify talents you never thought you had. This particular exercise shows I can convey emotions I am feeling and activate the same emotions in my audience. Now at this point of my life, I had no idea what my life purpose was, but pieces of the puzzle started to appear.

Aren't you becoming more and more curious? You should be, because can you now identify in your life the pieces of your puzzle coming together? Do you see there are no coincidences, only divine appointments? Wow, I am so excited for you!

One of the most powerful things I have learned writing this book is out of chaos can come order. Surrender to the present, be awake, and follow spirit. Some people think surrendering to a power greater than themselves is a sign of weakness. It is actually the opposite; it is a sign of strength. When you can pause for a few seconds before reacting to life, you can avoid a lot of heartache if your emotions are not involved. Remember, reacting from a place of survival is always about you, yourself, and you. You have no regard for others; you want what you want now. It is not a pretty sight. Have you ever videotaped yourself during an event? I have, and I didn't always like what I saw.

Whenever I have a situation that I feel I cannot solve alone, which is more or less everything, I surrender it to God. How exactly do I do that? I first pray and tell God the situation and why I need His help. Then I go to meditation. I create a space in my mind where I let go of self, my ego, and in that open space, I turn the person, place, or thing over to Him. The key is I have the faith and trust that He will take care of it. I then wait patiently for an intuitive thought from the Holy Spirit. I listen for direction and obediently take the necessary action. Sometimes, no action is needed. If you remember one thing about this teaching, it is God cannot produce miracles in your life if you don't take the necessary action.

God cannot produce miracles in your life if you don't do your part.

After forty-seven years of understanding this process, my prayers are usually answered within one to two days, but it can take months or even years to get an answer. I am going to devote a whole chapter on how to communicate with God and the necessary requirements for prayers to be answered and why.

Sometimes God takes care of me even when I don't ask. Let me tell you about one such event in 2008. I needed to buy a new car. My present vehicle was old and needed repairs. I certainly did not have the money to buy a new car but was looking for a used car that fit into my budget. It was about ten days before I was going to make the final decision on which car I was going to buy. Now every week, I call my parents religiously in England just to touch base and chat about current things. My dad came on the phone and said, "Could you use $10,000?"

"What?" I exclaimed. "I sure could! I am about to buy a car." So without me even praying about it, I got the money to buy a brand spanking new car off the car dealership lot. God is truly amazing. I give God all the glory and thank Him for His grace.

You too can have what I have if you do what I do. Read carefully, this book is full of treasures.

Good luck panning for gold nuggets. The bounty is limitless and, remember, each nugget is priceless, life-changing, and you can fly over the rainbow where dreams really do come true.

CHAPTER 15

Pack Light, You're Flying

We are now in 2009 and life is becoming increasingly more balanced. I now have three years of sobriety.

One of the greatest adventures I have loved my whole life is travelling overseas. I wanted to go on a trip, but where? I asked God to direct me to find a trip that would be ideal. I was in the locker room of my gym and noticed a flyer on the board advertising a yoga retreat to Peru. The group would be small, no more than twelve, and we would stay on a local plantation and eat vegetarian food for the week. We would be taken to Machu Picchu, and the trip was organized around the summer solstice in June.

Now I had never been on an airline flight sober. I would also be taking the trip alone, there would be no other alcoholic to watch my back. *Hm, I am going to pray about this.*

The result was I packed my bags; I was going on an adventure. Whoopee! Now I will really have to test my faith. Can I stay sober? Of course I can, if I use my tool bag and trust God.

Travelling there would take two connecting flights and about fifteen hours total air flight. I don't like long flights because I am never able to sleep and have a really hard time occupying myself. However, that is part of the package, so I put on my big girl panties and went for it.

I was met at the airport by the local guide and driven to my lodgings. The place where we were staying was beautiful. It was a yoga retreat built on a large plot of land. It was remote, private, and peaceful. They gave us our guest keys. The name on the front of my bedroom door meant "royal quilt." All the other guests had names of flowers on the front of their doors.

My room was delightful. A queen-sized bed, bathroom, and exquisite decorations everywhere. Now this is living.

We would gather in the dining room for dinner and we were serviced the most colorful, delicious, homegrown vegetable dishes. There were about twelve of us around the table. There were four couples and four single people. They were all from America. We talked and talked. Everyone was so excited to be in Peru.

I retired to bed around 11:00 p.m., and when I got into my bed, I had a wonderful surprise—a hot water bottle. What a special touch! I cuddled up to it. I got a warm fuzzy feeling all over my body.

Everyone would get up early to do yoga in the morning and then go to breakfast. The smell of freshly brewed coffee and warm homemade muffins delighted the senses. When I got to the dining room, I could hardly believe my eyes when I saw all the different foods and freshly squeezed juices just waiting for us to devour.

Our group had the yoga center to ourselves, and I felt so privileged to be a part of this wonderful adventure. Each morning, the tour guide would tell us the daily schedule. We visited many local sites, and at the end of the day, we would be taken to a local market. At the market, there were all kinds of things that could be purchased including homemade jewelry.

I remember one market in particular. All the vendors were arranged in a kind of horseshoe configuration. I walked around, looking at all the different wares. When I got to the farthest table, I stopped and looked at some of the homemade necklaces. I noticed there were three somewhat ill-kept children playing in the corner. I did not see anything I wanted to buy and turned to walk away when suddenly, a man appeared who had only one leg. I immediately realized it was the children's father. He looked at me with anticipation that I would buy something. There was no way I was going to leave now.

I picked out a necklace which needed to be shortened so it hung correctly around my neck. While I was waiting for the man to alter the length, I played with the children. I took pictures of them with my camera and showed them how they looked on the screen. They giggled and laughed. We held hands and I taught them "ring around the roses." I went into my imaginary world while I was skipping and dancing with the children. My imaginary world is where time stands still, I am fully present, and my heart is full of joy.

I gave each of the children a coin. I gave the father extra money for the necklace. Before I left, I said to the children, "Come and give me a big hug!" They all ran up to me, one grabbing on my leg and the other two hugging me so tightly they did not want to let go.

As I walked away from the marketplace, I turned around, and every vendor and person in that area was waving at me. Wow, what a feeling to be a stranger in a foreign country but not be a stranger at all! This is one of the points I am trying to convey in this book. We are all connected; there is no space or time between each and every person. We are one and we must connect energetically so we all benefit and save the world.

The town I was in was called Cusco. There was a town square, and I mentioned before it was the summer solstice. Peruvians had gathered from all the different towns in Peru to celebrate the event. They wore the most colorful, carefully decorated headdresses. Their clothes were the traditional clothing of the country. They would walk in a circle around the square. Some would dance, some would sing, but the energy of joy and celebration filled the air.

Also in the square were hundreds of children trying to sell you their handmade wooden animals. It was very sad. If they did not sell something that day, they simply did not eat. They were dirty and had shabby clothing, and most had no shoes. Peru is a third world country, and to realize what I have gives me overflowing gratitude.

In the square was a beautiful little church which I wanted to visit, but they did not allow tourists to enter. Now did I tell you I am tenacious? And if I want to do something, I can always find a way to accomplish the task. I waited until the service at 6:00 p.m. for mass where they cannot refuse anyone to enter. I walked into the church and sat down amongst all the locals. I am very familiar with how to present myself in a church in another country. I wore a long shirt, a blouse that covers my shoulders, and a scarf on my head. I acted very humble and always got on my knees and prayed. I thanked God for my life, my sobriety, my family, and the opportunity to really live life before I died. I asked to do His will always and let me be of service wherever I go.

The statues in the church were incredible. All the Peruvians were dressed in their Sunday best. I am never afraid of venturing into unfamiliar surroundings, but I am always acutely aware of who is around me and use my discernment at all times to sense if I am safe. The service was powerful. Of course, I didn't understand a word they said, but my senses picked up the energy. Did you know that your body can sense a situation a lot more accurately than your intellectual mind if you are in the present moment?

The next day, our group was going to travel north to visit Machu Picchu, which is an Incan citadel set high in the Andes Mountains in Peru, above the Urubamba River Valley. Built in the fifteenth century and later abandoned, it is renowned for its sophisticated dry-stone walls that fuse huge blocks without the use of mortar, intriguing buildings that play on astronomical alignments and panoramic views. Its exact former use remains a mystery.

I remember distinctly working through the entryway and being awestruck with the size of the enormous structure. We walked all around it with our guide. She had plenty of amazing stories and facts about the site. They would sacrifice animals at the altar to appease the gods.

Now this was the day before summer solstice. After the initial tour, we were free to roam around. I decided to walk up a very long steep hill so I could have a bird's-eye view of the magnificent Machu Picchu. It looked even more impressive from up above. It was built between three mountains, and how in the world did they get all that building material up there to build it? There are more than 150 buildings ranging from baths and houses to temples and sanctuaries.

We arrived back at our local hotel for the night. The next day, we were on our own to explore the town. However, I overheard the guide saying she was going back to Machu Picchu the next day with a couple of people from the group but she was not going to announce it. She wanted to be there when the sun came up on the day of the summer solstice. So what do you think I did? I followed them. She went into a secret room inside the structure and put crystals in the open space which you would have considered a window opening. I followed them in. What were they going to say? Go away? I don't think so.

We all waited patiently for the sunrise. As the sun grew higher in the sky, the light hit the crystals in such a way that the room was filled with intense light. The light was sparkling and rays emulated from the crystals in such a way that you felt the very presence of God. I fell to my knees and the energy in my body was so powerful. I cried uncontrollably for thirty minutes.

At the end, I felt this amazing spiritual shift in my consciousness. The other people looked at me as if I was an alien from another planet. No one hugged me or came close to me to console me after shedding all those tears. That experience was what made that vacation unforgettable.

I had mentioned before that everyone went to yoga first thing in the morning. Not me. I took my coffee and went into the garden and sat under the Pachamama tree.

Pachamama is a goddess revered by the indigenous people of Peru. She is also known as the Earth Mother.

I sat under the trees in the garden and talked to God every morning. He shared His wisdom, and I wrote it down in a journal. Below are some extracts from that journal.

> You must show kindness always. The peace I give you, you must give to others. You must focus on the innocence of the world, not the imperfections. Remember, I am in all things. To receive my healing, you must completely let go. Believe and you will receive. Do not question me. There is a purpose to everything. You are special because of your faith. To know me is to won-

der. Everything you need is within. Guidance is everywhere, because I am in all things.

I will give you strength—physical, emotional, and spiritual endurance.

I will give you power—incredible intuition and foresight.

I will give you courage to carry out the service asked of you.

I have about twenty pages of downloads and I still read them often.

One day I was sitting in the garden, and a man appeared. He was short in stature and he wore a poncho and a hat that looked like a scarecrow would wear. He was carrying a sack over his shoulder. He looked at me and smiled and nodded his head at me. Who was he?

I learned he was Don Bonito, the second highest spiritual healer in Peru. He had travelled by foot for two days over mountains and pastures to come to the center to give us personal healings. Oh boy, we were definitely in for a surprise.

That evening, we all gathered around a fireplace, and our guide introduced us to the wise healer. Then each of us was asked individually to go up to him and personally introduce ourselves. Each person Don Bonito met was welcomed with a graceful handshake. Then it was my turn to go up and shake his hand. As soon as I got close to him, he literally grabbed hold of me and gave me the biggest hug. Well, what a welcome! He must have intuitively felt my energy and felt akin to me.

He did a tea leaf reading for each of us. The reading was done indoors in a very small room with no open windows. I had told him about my history with alcohol abuse. When he turned the teacup over and the leaves fell to the table, one leaf literally flew a foot in the air and landed a great distance away from the other leaves. He told me my alcoholism had left me. I thought that was nice, but I was never going to test that theory out.

The next day, we visited a local school. It was situated in the beautiful mountains of Peru. There were over a hundred children attending the school. We visited their classrooms and saw some of the crafts they were working on. They were full of excitement about our visit and wanted to show us everything. Of course, school supplies were scarce. They also had no working toilets. The lunch they gave us consisted of potatoes that had been cooked outside on the ground.

I loved Peru. It was so interesting. I got a new perspective on my life. It is amazing how small one's life can become until you go to another country and your vision opens up in ways unimaginable. I felt creative, energetic, and full of awe about my life's journey.

There were a lot more wonderful experiences I had in Peru that I have not mentioned. However, this is not a travel guide; it's about what kind of experiences changed me along my journey.

I have so many more adventures I want to tell you about. Are you ready to hear about the next country I visited and how God told me my life purpose?

I think that is a definite yes.

CHAPTER 16

Up on the Mountaintop, Hear Me Whisper

The next country I visited was Egypt in 2010. Exploring this country was probably one of my favorite trips. I would love to invite you into my living room and show you all my pictures from Egypt. I would love to tell you all about the fascinating adventures I took and all the people I met. However, that is not what this book is about. It is about my divine encounters and how my life changed forever. Let me tell you, I have had plenty of them.

Someone I knew had taken this trip to Egypt and said how amazing it was and that I should go. I went through the same travel agent and was assured I would be safe. Basically, it was a guide and myself exploring Egypt. No lines, no going through security, we could simply hop here and there quite swiftly.

The first church I visited in Cairo was Saint Virginia Mary's Orthodox Church, also known as the hanging church because it is suspended over a passage. I got on my knees and prayed in the church, and the message I received from God was, "You will be my light in the world."

Interesting, I thought.

Then I was taken to Saints Sergius and Bacchus Church, the oldest Coptic church in Egypt. This is the church where Joseph, Mary, and Jesus escaped to when Herod ordered the firstborn of every family to be killed. It was hard to believe I was in a church that was originally built 2000 years ago.

I spent a week on a riverboat on the Nile. It was an unbelievable experience. I had a wonderful room with a full window so I could lie on my bed and watch the world go by.

There was a wonderful buffet at breakfast, lunch, and dinner. It was a feast extravaganza. All my senses were alive and energized from the anticipation of indulging in all the different delicacies. Food that was beautifully presented, fresh fruit and vegetables grown locally, the smell of tastefully prepared meats and all the waiters anxiously waiting to serve us—now that was heaven on earth!

I always like sitting in a dining room at a table for two. I love people watching. My mind is totally disengaged, there are no thoughts running through my head. I am living fully in the present moment and totally at peace with the world. It is very hard for other people to understand that most people like to socialize with others.

At dinner, I would always sit with a group of people and talk about the daily events. I say I am an extroverted introvert. Of course, people who enjoy their own company are good company for others.

I visited all kinds of temples, sanctuaries, churches, and local towns. I loved every minute of it, and Little Anne is always the center of attention wherever she goes. Big Anne being the introvert and Little Anne being the extrovert, we make an excellent team.

One place I wanted to visit was Mount Sinai, the mountain where Moses received The Ten Commandments. It was about a three-hour drive north from where we were, but my intuition told me I needed to go. The hotel where I was staying had no safe in the room, and the bedroom door did not lock, so I decided to carry all my valuables in my backpack that day.

I was to meet my local guide at twelve midnight and walk five miles up the mountain to the very top. At around 6:00 a.m., we were expected to see the sunrise.

The guide looked like he lived in the mountains. He spoke no English, and I am sure he was not a licensed guide. My intuition became acute and I scanned him for any sense of danger. My danger monitor read negative for any sense of warning regarding my safety.

We started walking up the hill in complete darkness. Only the stars shone brightly in the sky to illuminate our path. We walked and walked up the very steep mountain. It was necessary to be in good physical shape to accomplish the climb. We were to arrive at the top around 5:30 a.m. However, I am a very fast walker, and at around 2:30 a.m., we had almost arrived at our destination.

My guide stopped by a cave and invited me in. There were three men inside, and immediately my heart started beating really hard. Oh no, I am in a cave with four men I don't know, and all my money and jewelry is in my backpack which is on my back! I started praying. They told me to rest and take a nap because we had arrived so early for the sunrise. *Hell no, I have to get out of here!* So I instructed my guide to walk me the rest of way up to the top of the mountain.

We arrived at 2:45 a.m.. We had almost three hours to wait for the anticipated glorious sunrise. It was very cold, the wind was blowing hard, and we were in complete darkness.

My guide came close to me and shared his blanket. A blue-eyed, blonde haired female, small in stature and unable to talk to her companion, was cuddled on top of a mountain with a native Egyptian who was probably living in poverty. Don't tell me all countries cannot unite if both nationalities can show mutual respect, love, and share a common goal with each other.

I don't know if you noticed another gift God gave me. It is no matter what country I am in, there is a natural bond formed between me and the natives of that country.

Be humble always, be honest, have compassion, and see cultural differences disappear. There is goodness in every human being. When ego disappears, spirits unite for the common good.

While we were waiting, I used the time wisely to talk to God. I asked him, "How did Moses know to come to this mountain?"

God answered, "He heard my voice."

I asked him, "Why did you want me to come to Mount Sinai?"

God replied, "Because I need to give you a special message."

"What is the message," I asked.

Now it is a good job I was sitting down, because this was God's reply: "You will speak to hundreds, thousands, and millions of people about me."

I said, "Who, me?" I thought that was a very tall order, but who am I to question God? Tell God your plans and give him a good laugh!

I took in the information and know from previous experiences, if the service seems impossible, just be quiet, patient, and listen for instructions. No point in wasting my time and energy future tripping. God is always in control, no matter what the circumstances.

Around 4:00 a.m., a group of African Americans arrived. They were dressed in the brightest most colorful clothing you could imagine. They all held hands in a circle and started singing to the Lord. Some got on their knees and gave praises and thanks to the mighty Father. I was simply awestruck. It was the most magnificent ceremony I had ever seen worshipping the Father.

Around 5:30 a.m., I looked behind me and there were about 150 people waiting patiently for the much anticipated spectacular sunrise.

My heart was beating so fast I could feel it through my shirt. Then suddenly, a small ray of light appeared on the horizon. Everyone was speechless and no one muttered a word.

The light became brighter, and suddenly, you could see the shape of the sun. All the mountains around where glowing with a golden light. It was as if the sun had given energy to every living thing. The sun grew bigger, brighter, and more powerful with every second. It was totally mesmerizing.

When the sun had risen above the horizon, my guide instructed me to hand him my camera and pose in front of the sunrise. He told me to put my hand out as if I was carrying something. When I looked at the image on my camera, I saw a silhouette of myself carrying the sun in my hand. Now that was an incredible photograph!

We finally made our descent down the mountain, five miles down, and my knees felt the pain. I thanked my guide and was met by my original guide from the travel agency.

We started to drive off to our next destination. The Egyptian trip was so varied and interesting on all levels. One stopover included visiting a local village where I got to hold a baby crocodile.

I booked a couple of extra days in Cairo and asked my guide if he would take me to some sights I had not already seen. I would pay him for the extra time. He took me to the most magnificent synagogue I had ever seen. I have seen quite a few on my worldly travels but nothing that compared to this one. It had thousands of lights illuminating the inside. The floor was made up of intricate mosaic tiles.

Egypt was an absolutely incredible country, and I got to learn what my life purpose was directly from the voice of God.

It had been six years since I had last visited my parents in England, so I decided to pay them a visit on my way home.

When I got off the airplane to meet them, I was physically and emotionally exhausted. They greeted me with this response: "Oh my God, you look terrible. Your hair is not blonde enough and you don't look like your photographs." I never heard the words, "It's great to see you, Anne, we have missed you." If there had been a plane available to take me straight home to America, I would have turned around and got on it. But alas, there wasn't.

The visit with my parents was the usual, and I will spare you the details. However, I do want to tell you one thing. The most priceless, loving, God-given gift could be standing right before you. However, if you are blinded by your own shattered ego, you will miss the blessing.

Focus on the negative things in a person, and that's all you will see. Focus on the positive things, and the person appears to be a totally different human being.

That's why in life, most people really like me; in fact, most people love me. However, people who are unhappy, stuck in life, and have no joy in their heart simply hate me. Not only that, they will go out of their way to try and cause me harm.

The lesson from this story is I did not put any boundaries up with my parents. I was open, vulnerable, and as a result, I got hurt emotionally yet again.

Doing the same thing over and over again, expecting different results, is called insanity. I simply didn't expect my parents to continually emotionally abuse me. However, if they had always treated me that way, why would they treat me any different?

When someone continues with destructive behavior, year after year, and no one points out the harm they are causing, how are they supposed to know the chaos and pain they are causing? It is like the joke when the wife says to her husband, "If you loved me, you would know what I want." Really, "I love you for better and for worse, and you had better be a mind reader." High expectations. don't you think? But I am the first to admit it. I did that exact thing with my children's father.

Pause and listen carefully to what you are saying to yourself and others. Awareness of the actions we take and how they affect others is the beginning of enlightenment and higher consciousness.

Well, I hope that chapter made you think about your dreams, visions, and possible internal messages that are leading you to your life purpose.

Amen.

CHAPTER 17

Abracadabra, Believe It or Not

The year 2011 was a stormy year. My daughter was going to be entering her senior year in high school. She wanted me to move back to Fairfield so we could live together for that year before she went to college. I reluctantly moved back to Fairfield from Napa at the beginning of the year.

I say "reluctantly," because I had too many drunk memories in Fairfield and did not want to be reminded. But before I moved, God sent me on a scavenger hunt. During meditation, He said He had a message for me and I had to go to Goodwill to find it. Oh boy, here I go. I could not open the door to Goodwill fast enough. My whole body felt like electricity was running through it from head to toe. My heart was beating so fast I could feel it through my shirt.

I looked everywhere, looking behind objects, under bookcases, behind miscellaneous items but could not find a possible message anywhere. Then all of a sudden, I saw a picture of Christ holding a man close to his chest. I looked closer at the picture frame and saw a piece of paper stuck in the bottom of the frame. I shouted with ecstasy, "There's the message!" The paper read Matthew 25:21.

I ran home to open the Bible to read the scripture. It said, "Well done, good and faithful servant! You have been faithful with a few things; I will put you in charge of many things. Come and share your master's happiness!"

Wow, I was speechless. I wasn't sure what to think, but I knew it was a piece of the puzzle to my amazing journey with God.

Benjamin helped me move, and he was fantastic. There were so many boxes to go through and get rid of things I did not need. He stayed focused from beginning to end.

It took a couple of months for me to finally get settled in my new apartment in Fairfield. There was definitely some tension between Sarah and myself, which is normal when families try and unite after going through trauma.

One of my lifelong goals is to do a "living amends" to both my children. It can take years for them to trust you again. I was lucky that my children separated Mom and Mom plus drinking. Drinking causes alcoholics to have a Jekyll and Hyde personality. When I was in my disease, my son noticed when I took one gulp of alcohol, my personality changed.

I started going to a new twelve-step meeting in Fairfield, but the people there were not very friendly. I had called several women from the meeting, but they never returned my call. I was extremely angry. Any alcoholic should always return another alcoholic's call. Why? Because you may be saving their life. They may be on the verge of taking a drink. Now for me, to take a drink is to literally die. When people relapse, they pick up exactly where they left off.

God kept prompting me, for some reason, to announce to the step meeting my resentment about their conduct. I kept trying to avoid taking the action, because I knew what the disruption would cause. I would also become completely distanced from the group.

The anger inside of me grew bigger and bigger with every meeting I attended. Finally, the straw broke the camel's back. I let rip and everyone's jaw fell to the floor. Remember the story about the little boy who states the obvious? Well, that is exactly what I did. I believe it is very important to stand up and point out injustice because as a result, you may be saving the next person who needs help. Things are never the same when light is brought into the darkness.

It's never a good thing when you get angry in any situation, because you get an "emotional hangover." These can manifest in headaches, low energy, and emotional imbalance. Yuck!

However, a few days later, I got a call from a man who had heard my frustration voiced at the meeting. He told me to go to Benicia to find a sponsor. This is a town about twenty minutes from Fairfield. I immediately said to myself, "That is such an odd thing for that to happen. It must be a 'God shot.'" That means God wants me to follow that man's suggestion.

I decided to go to a Benicia twelve-step meeting with the intent on finding the best sponsor possible to help me grow in sobriety. I met a couple of ladies I knew from a previous program. Both had around twenty-six-years sobriety. They told me Theresa was the best sponsor they had ever worked with and she would be at the meeting next week.

The next week came, and I waited patiently in the meeting for Theresa to arrive. She sat right next to me. I introduced myself and asked her if she could sponsor me. Her response was, "I am sorry, I have too many sponsees right now." However, right in the middle of the sentence, she abruptly stopped, paused, and turned to face me. She said in a somewhat robotic way, "Why don't you call me tomorrow and we can talk?"

I smiled and thought, *God is always in control.*

Theresa became my sponsor and is still my sponsor today. She has definitely changed my life. God continually works through her, guiding and teaching me to become the woman I and God want me to be. Remember, I cannot be a good servant if I am carrying a ton of garbage around with me. I need to see the truth, not a distorted truth, so I can make wise decisions about my life.

One of the most important pieces of work I have done for personal growth is the *12 Steps of Codependency*. I think the book was written for me.

The definition of codependency is an emotional and behavioral condition that affects an individual's ability to have a healthy, mutually satisfying relationship. It is also known as "relationship addiction," because people with codependency often form or maintain relationships that are one-sided, emotionally destructive, and/ or abusive.

Does that sound familiar? Especially with our children. We want to save them from falling. However, we are actually doing more harm than good. If they don't fall, they will not learn the lessons they need to live life on life's terms.

When you come from a dysfunctional family, it is like walking through life, trying to miss the potholes that are invisible. Another way of saying it is walking through a minefield trying to avoid explosions. My friend, I lived that life; it is no fun whatsoever.

I am driven to write this book so, hopefully, I can give you a road map which indicates where the potholes could be hidden before you step in them. After reading this book, I truly want you to get up from your chair, run down the street, and kiss a stranger.

It is around February 2011, and I had been attending a local church. They mentioned baptizing people on Easter Sunday. I thought I want to get baptized, especially on the day Jesus rose from the dead.

I had disappeared from Fairfield for the last six years or so. No one knew what had happened to me. In the pews, that morning, were a lot of old faces. Boy, were they in for a surprise!

I stepped up to the podium and started giving my testimony. My friend who was in the audience listening said there was a halo of light surrounding me. She said I looked like an angel.

My testimony was very powerful, and even the pastor's mouth was hanging open. I am constantly amazed with my life's journey and how God uses me for service. People who had known me in the past came up to me after the baptism and hugged me.

When I got home that afternoon, I turned to Benjamin and said, "Watch what the devil will do to me."

It was about two days later when Sarah got up to get ready for school. I was having a hard time getting out of bed because of my allergies. When I walked into the kitchen, Sarah jumped on top of me, held me down on the floor, and a voice came screaming out of her. The voice said, "I am going to kill you, I am going to kill you! You have always been in my way! You know it's just a matter of time."

I got up, and Sarah jumped on me again, and the voice said, "I am going to kill you!"

Now I am fully aware that the devil will use anything or anyone to deter me, but I had never seen him enter somebody's body before and talk to me in such a violent way. Scary.

Being a spiritual warrior is definitely challenging. The greater your purpose, the greater the opposing force. However God's power is greater than any other force in the universe. I have the faith that God inside of me will always be triumphant. If I did not believe that, I probably would not get out of bed in the morning.

Sarah went to live with her father. It was very unfortunate because I had moved from Napa to Fairfield so we could live together.

The next couple of months, I had nightmares and would start screaming in the middle of the night. The episode with Sarah triggered my post-traumatic stress syndrome. I always felt like I took three steps forward and two steps back. I was very discouraged because I was already having trouble sleeping.

Benjamin would come over on the weekend and had to sometimes calm me down in the middle of the night. When I woke up, I didn't know where I was.

It was getting time to take my next vacation. I had already booked it at the beginning of the year and could not have foreseen my present dilemma. I was about to embark on a river cruise to Russia. The boat would sail from Moscow to St. Petersburg along the Volga river.

Travelling from California to Moscow was one of the most grueling travel itineraries I had ever experienced. Most trips from California to my destination took around twenty-four hours, but this took longer. Remember, I had not been sleeping well before the trip.

When I arrived in Moscow, I told God, "I am so exhausted. I don't know if I have the strength to go find my luggage and lift it off the conveyor belt." Of course, I didn't have any choice. After I had gone through customs, I took the elevator down to the ground level in search of Baggage Claim. The airport was very congested, and people were rushing to and forth to get in and out of the airport. There was a main further fare where people were walking. I noticed right in the middle of the congested crowd a piece of luggage. I thought, *What an odd place for a bag to be placed. Why had someone not moved it to the proper location where some poor person would be looking for it?* It was standing upright and it had not been knocked down with the chaotic stream of people. As I looked closer at the suitcase, I said to myself, "That looks like my suitcase! But that is impossible!" My curiosity grew stronger and I walked up to the luggage to take a closer look. It was my suitcase! How in the world had it gotten there?

Now I have seen God produce miracles time after time, but really! God placed that suitcase there right in the path where I needed to walk to exit the airport. This is one of those times when I would say to myself, "Don't tell anybody. They will never believe you and consider you a complete nutcase." However, I came to the conclusion I am already an oddball, so why not include it in my autobiography with God?

Russia was an absolutely fascinating country. The stories about the czars were unbelievably intriguing, a lot like English royalty. Queen Elizabeth I chopped off the head of Mary, Queen of Scots, because she was jealous of her.

One story they told us was about a young boy in line to become the next czar of Russia. His mother took him to a remote village to hide him. She feared he was in danger of being killed by the next predecessor to become the czar.

They found out where the boy was living and a posse of soldiers went to the village and killed the young boy. They then cut out all the tongues of the villagers so they could not tell anyone what happened. The man who ordered the slaughter then became the next czar.

Of course, one of the most gruesome stories from Russia was the slaughter of Czar Nicholas II and his family by left wing extremists. They made a movie about Anastasia who they suspected escaped the massacre.

One of our tours was to the oldest part of Moscow where several Russian Orthodox Churches were located, an area called Sergiev Posad. We visited several sites including The Trinity Cathedral. When everyone had completed the tour, we were given free time.

I went back into the cathedral to pray. I had my eyes closed, but I sensed someone walking toward me, and he or she stopped right in front of me. I thought, *How rude.* I opened my eyes and visually saw no one standing in front of me, but someone was there. I reached my hand out to try and touch it, but there was no physical form. I asked, "Who are you?" But I got no answer.

After I left the cathedral, I felt giddy and full of wonder, and for some unexplainable reason, I held my camera over my head, shooting at the sky. I am known to take, on average, around 1500 pictures during a vacation. Periodically during the day, I would look through my photos and delete all the ones I didn't want to keep. I had five minutes before the group was to gather together, so I decided to delete that last picture. To my absolute amazement, when I looked at the photo that had been shot randomly, there was a circle of white light with a dove in the center with its wings perfectly horizontal. In the Christian Bible, the dove represents the Holy Spirit and peace.

My interpretation of the event was God was reminding me He is ever-present in my life, that there is the trinity—God, Jesus, and the Holy Spirit. It would be a bit presumptuous of me to say Jesus was standing in front of me in the cathedral, but who knows? It might have been. The cathedral was call The Trinity.

I saw all kinds of amazing sights during my vacation to Russia, and it transformed me in many ways. One way was my gratitude for my freedom gained from God's wisdom, personal awareness of who I truly am, and my joyful heart.

Russians are an oppressed culture. They appear sad and weighed down from life. We talk about inherent pain bodies carried down from one generation to another. In World War II, Hitler burned down St. Petersburg and left everybody to die from starvation. This kind of pain can be passed down through several generations. They also had to live through hard cold winters.

During my stay in Russia, it was not uncommon to see men taking shots of vodka at 7:00 a.m. before going to work. Of course, it reminded me how I would drink vodka first thing in a morning. Addiction gave me no choice to say yes or no to taking a drink. The further away you are from your last drink, the closer you are to your next drink.

There is exactly a twelve-hour difference between California and Moscow. So if it's 4:00 a.m. in California, it is 4:00 p.m. in

Moscow. I simply never got acclimated to the time difference. There were times when I was really tired because I never seemed to get a good night's sleep.

I remember one evening going to dinner and deciding I could not be at a table where alcohol was being served. It wasn't that I needed to drink, but I was totally unbalanced emotionally and very unsure of my thought patterns and actions I might take. If I was at home, I would have gone to a meeting or, at the very least, talked to another alcoholic.

I chose to sit at a quiet table where no one else was sitting. A gentleman sat down opposite me. I noticed his wife was sitting on the opposite side of the boat, which I thought was rather odd. I said, "I hope you are not drinking alcohol tonight. I am a recovering alcoholic and feel uneasy." He reassured me by saying he was drinking a diet soda.

Now there were 200 passengers on board, and this man chose to not sit with his wife but sit at a table where only I was sitting. We started talking, but I was only communicating out of politeness. I wanted to be left alone.

About fifteen minutes into the conversation, he said to me, "Don't you people have some sort of prayer you say about serenity and courage?"

I said. "Yes, the Serenity Prayer."

He said, "Why don't you recite it to me?"

I had to pause for a moment because I forgot how it started. Then I suddenly remembered. "God, give me the serenity to accept the things I cannot change, the courage to change the things I can, and the wisdom to know the difference."

I felt an immediate relief. The man instructed me to say the prayer two more times. What a difference a prayer can make. The interaction between myself and the man; was it coincidence? Or did God put him there? I think you know the answer.

My journey with God has given me the most mysterious, mystical, unimaginable, unexplainable, and wondrous life I could ever have imagined. I hope, one day, you truly can experience His amazing grace.

CHAPTER 18

Don't Be in the Wrong Place at the Right Time

I arrived home from Russia on a Sunday evening. I was glad to be home and sleep in my own bed. Everyone was so pleased to see me. It is great to see my loved ones smiling faces.

Two days later, I was scheduled to go into the women's jail in Napa. I always looked forward to seeing the ladies so I could give them my experience, strength, and hope. I would always get into my car at 7:00 p.m. and be at the jail at 7:30 p.m. I am always on time for meetings, especially when going into the jail. If I am not on time, I don't get to go in. I had never missed a meeting in eight years.

It was Tuesday evening, around 6:45. I was ready to leave my apartment to go to Napa when I got a call from the jail. They informed me the meeting had been cancelled because the women did not want a meeting. That did not make any sense because it was mandatory for the women in work furlough to attend a meeting. The staff at the jail where insistent I was not to come in that evening.

So around 6:50 p.m., I put my purse and car keys down. I took my shoes off and sat down on the couch and turned on the TV.

At around 7:05 p.m., I got a knock at my front door. A lady was standing there and she said, "Did you see what happened at 7: p.m.?"

I replied, "No."

She said, "A tree fell and demolished your car."

"What?" I looked over the balcony to see my car. The wind had been blowing extremely hard over the last couple of days. And yes, there was a tree on the top of my car that had collapsed the roof. If I had gotten into my car at 7:00 p.m., I would have either died or been badly hurt. God is always protecting me wherever I go. Always give thanks to God and testify his power to others.

Now to the atheists and agnostics reading this book. At this point, you must be at least believing something or someone is guiding, loving, and protecting me, right?

So Christmas and New Year came and went. That is my favorite time of the year. I wish it could snow on Christmas Eve in Fairfield California, just to make it more festive.

We are now in 2012, and I decided I needed to go see a therapist. I was still having panic attacks from the incident last Easter. I searched for a therapist who specializes in Eye Movement Desensitization and Reprocessing. I eventually found one in Davies. I made an appointment with her and she was very informative. They use EMDR on soldiers who come back from the war with PTSD.

She took me back to my worst memory of being traumatized. When I am feeling my body react to the trauma, a pulse is passed from ear to ear. The idea is to keep going back to the memory, and you should react less and less, and eventually, a new memory replaces the old. She, however, wanted God to guide me through the process. I want to tell you about one particular session.

The memory we went back to was when I was around ten years old and I was in the kitchen in the house in Rochdale. My mother had just told me the best years of her life were before I was born. I sat quietly, waiting for God to guide me. I was sitting with my back to my mother. In my vision, God came up through the floor, grasped my hand, and took me up to the ceiling. He said, "Now look down at your mother. You have a choice. The life you have with me now or you can live your life over and have an amazing relationship with her. What is your choice?"

I replied, "That is a no brainer. This life with you, of course." But then I retaliated and said, "But it's not fair for a little girl to wait at the window every night for her father to come home. He never paid me any attention."

God replied, "I don't know what you are complaining about. You wanted to change the world, didn't you? So you have to go through the hard lessons to become that spiritual leader."

"Change the world!" I exclaimed. "That's an impossible task. What was I thinking? Are you sure I said that?" That was a stupid question. I was talking to God.

There were many other sessions, but that was the most significant one. The therapist said in her twenty-five years of practicing, she had never met anyone who had such an amazing relationship with God.

Me and Benjamin have an ongoing phrase that makes us laugh. I say, "I can't believe He chose me." The original person who said that was a Buddhist monk.

I don't know if the therapy sessions really helped with my PTSD. However, they definitely gave me another piece of the puzzle to my life's purpose.

Sometime during 2013, I went to hear a talk by Marianne Williamson. It was in the Marin area, about forty-five minutes from where I lived. At the end of her speech, she would allow people to come up to the podium and ask questions. I went up and announced to the audience I was looking for like-minded souls in my area.

A lady from Fairfield came up to me after the seminar and gave me her business card. She told me to call her some time so we could get coffee and chat.

I called her a couple of weeks later, and we met at Starbucks. She told me she was a member of a group of women who, through inspirational speaking, were bringing their message to the world. In fact, she informed me there were ten women speaking on stage the next day, and she was one of them. She encouraged me to come and listen to the presentations.

I intuitively knew that God wanted me to go. What were the chances of our meeting in Starbucks one day before the speaking event?

The next day, I was introduced to the owner of the organization and she welcomed me with open arms. It was extremely interesting watching and listening to all the speakers. Each one had a different way of presenting themselves and the mission they were passionate about.

Once a year, they had a competition where women would compete against each other for a chance to speak in the January showcase presentations. In this event, friends and the general public would buy tickets to attend.

In order for you to be a part of the group of women, you had to be available for all the practices. My friend said the owner of the group made no exceptions. I had—unfortunately or fortunately, depending how you look at things—booked my next vacation to Australia. This would mean I would not be available for all the practices before the competition. Remember what Mark taught me—no doesn't always mean no.

I went up to talk to the group's leader and asked if I could join the group of ladies competing for the event in January. I informed her I would be going to Australia for three weeks during the period where they would be practicing for the competition.

She said, "That's okay."

Her business partner turned to her and said, "Why did you say that?"

She said, "I don't know, spirit made me say it."

If God is on my side, who can be against me?

So off I went to Australia. It was a very long flight, but fortunately, the seat next to me was vacant. I was on an airbus, and the plane was amazing. You could watch, on the screen in front of you, the plane taking off and landing. There were all kinds of movies to watch. There was even a menu for each meal. My eyes must have been as large as saucers because the man sitting near me looked at me like I was an alien from another planet. He announced he always travelled on an airbus. Well excuse me! I hadn't had the privilege before.

Well, I have something very funny to tell you. I booked a trip for singles to Australia. I asked the travel agent, "Where are the other singles?"

She said, "You are the only one that booked the trip."

"Huh! Don't you think you should have told me?"

She apparently did not think so.

I arrived in Sydney, spent a couple of days there, then flew to Uluru/Ayers Rock in the desert. We camped in tents under the star-filled sky. I then flew to Cairns to dive in the Great Barrier Reef and back to Sydney.

Now let's talk about my spiritual experiences in Australia. The trip to Uluru/Ayers Rock involved camping for three days in tents. We went on daily hikes to three different rock formations. First day, Uluru/Ayers Rock; second day, Kata Tjuta; and last day, King's Canyon. These rock formations are gigantic, and they started forming 500 million years ago when the Australian continent was being formed. So if you believe everything has energy (even enormous rock formations) like I do, can you imagine the energies that have been absorbed over the millions of years?

On our first hike to Uluru/Ayers Rock, we went into different caves and saw original aboriginal paintings. We also saw delicate plant life growing along the side of the caves.

At the end of the hike, I meditated and felt this feeling of being pulled into the rock. The experience was amazing, and my inner voice spoke clearly and precisely indicating all the power I needed was within. The deeper I went inside myself, the intensity of the power would increase. I felt like I was unstoppable and that I could achieve anything I put my mind to.

That night, I slept in a swag and went to sleep staring at a full moon and the twinkling stars. What an experience!

The next day, we hiked to Kata Tjuta. It was raining, but that did not dampen my enthusiasm. The rock formations were gigantic and majestic. I had actually never hiked on such large rock formations before. Everyone bundled up with rainproof gear and started off very enthusiastically on our new adventure.

The guide was very knowledgeable and helped some of us climb over the slippery rocks. The weather reminded me of England—foggy and damp. There were about ten people on the walk.

Toward the end of the hike, I again held back from the group and meditated for ten minutes. The gigantic rock again gave me the feeling of being pulled toward it. This time, an image of a lion appeared, and I sensed him pulling me into his eyes. Then an elephant appeared, and all kinds of different animals one after the other. They appeared so close to my face. They startled me, and again, I felt like I disappeared into their eyes. My inner voice told me life was precious and a gift not to be taken for granted. We are all connected to everyone, the animals, and every other living thing.

On the last day, we hiked King's Canyon. That hike was the most spectacular of the three hikes and will remain etched in my memory forever. The climb up was very strenuous, but what an amazing view from the top. We actually walked all around the top rim of the mountain range. King's Canyon is almost one hundred meters high, and right in the center in the bottom of the canyon is a sacred ceremonial oasis called the Garden of Eden. There were beautiful trees, brushes, and flowers surrounding a small pond, and all kinds of different birds flew in and out.

I looked at my reflection in the water, and my inner voice said, "You must bring your light to the darkness." It is harder today to illuminate any part of the world, because fear seems to be more prominent in all cultures.

I then travelled to Cairns and was fortunate enough to scuba dive in the Great Barrier Reef. The coral reef was remarkable, and I swam around effortlessly like a mermaid. I saw giant turtles and shoals of different colored fish swimming in front of my face, some brightly colored red, others orange, and some multicolored.

I loved visiting Australia. In fact, one of the highlights of the trip was going to see a musical at the Sydney Opera House on the day of Thanksgiving in America.

On a sidenote, a few weeks before I went to Australia, I went to my usual thrift store in my hometown. I go every Thursday, because everything in the store is 50 percent off. On one particular Thursday when I walked into the store, I saw a black sequined dress hanging from a clothes rack all by itself. The hem was cut into a jagged pattern. I said to myself, "Oh, that would be a perfect dress to wear going to a Cinderella ball." I had no occasion to wear the dress, but with a $400 original tag on the dress and the sale price being ten dollars, I had to buy it.

A month later when I talked to my travel agent about the itinerary for Australia, I mentioned I wanted to go to the Sydney Opera House and watch a musical. She said she would look into it for me. When she got back to me, surprise, surprise, Cinderella was playing. I had great fun dressing up in my new black sequined dress and walked through the front door of the building with my head held high, thinking I was one of the cast members.

This time, I was definitely in the right place at the right time.

CHAPTER 19

Let God Drive the Bus. He Knows the Shortest Way to Your Destination

When I got home to the apartment, Nathan was moving out. He had decided to rent his own apartment in the complex. I was really sad but also relieved to get my own space back. I like everything in its place, and Nathan was definitely not as clean and tidy as I would have liked.

Unfortunately, while I was out of town, all the mailboxes got broken into and a check that I received every month was stolen. The money I receive is from an investment I made in a senior housing complex. I called the owner and he said my check could not be reissued. I basically lost that money. However, he mentioned, why don't you move into the complex? I could save a lot of money each month on rent.

Moving to those apartments saved me a whopping $650 a month. The extra savings paid for my yearly vacation.

Now back to the speaking competition. There were forty contestants competing to speak in an event called "A Celebration of Continued Success, Collaboration, and Making the World a Better Place in 2014."

I had not been able to attend some of the training sessions because I had been away on vacation, but I was ready and willing to do my presentation. The night of the auditions was nerve-racking.

There were about seven judges, and the room was full of people anxiously awaiting the participants to showcase their presentations.

My number, in the order of presentations, was toward the end of the competition which added to my anxiety, and of course, it seemed like forever before I was called to the stage. Once I got up there and started speaking, it seemed to effortlessly come together. I was thankful for the opportunity to voice my message to the judges and audience.

It was about a week later when we got the announcement who the three winners were. I was one of them and proud to be a part of "Voices of Leadership."

When the day arrived for the big event, everyone was really excited and invited as many friends and family as possible. There was a special guest speaker who was a global change agent and internationally renowned expert on higher purpose.

I was placed last in order of speaking presentations. Again, I prayed my nerves would not get the better of me. My heart was beating so hard and my hands were sweating. It was hard staying composed. You know the saying, "Never let them see you sweat?" Well, I thought for sure I was going to dissolve into the floor.

Finally, I was called to the stage. I stepped up to the microphone and was just about to start speaking when I totally forgot what to say. I was about to apologize to the audience that I was lost for words and needed to sit down. However, suddenly my mouth opened and words came out that I had no control over. My message flowed, my enthusiasm heightened, and I could see from the faces in the audience that I was connecting with them energetically. It was like time had stood still.

One woman's eyes were full of tears. Another woman appeared to be totally in a trance. The silence was encapsulating; you could have heard a pin drop. I could feel God's energy and we were united as one source, one power, one voice.

When I finished my speech, I gave a deep sigh of relief. I remember sitting down on a chair and saying silently, "Thank you, God, for being with me."

When I was leaving the event, many people came up to me, thanking me for my powerful message. I could not really remember the exact words that came out of my mouth, but I accomplished what God wanted me to do. My message was about human suffering and how God, in His grace, saved my life and gave me a new beginning.

Two ladies from the audience came up to me as I was leaving the building and said, "Who are you? When you talk, God's energy fills the whole room."

I politely said, "Anne Hayes."

They said, "You are definitely ready to go out in the world and become an inspirational speaker."

I smiled and thought to myself, *You ain't seen nothing yet, ladies. Isn't that right, God?*

I felt a warm feeling in my heart which conveyed this message from my heavenly Father: "I am always with you, my precious child; Be still and know I am God."

I did not know at the time, but there was a TV producer from a local station in Ukiah. She invited me to speak on her show early in 2015. My message was about "Fear verses Faith." I spoke for about twenty minutes, and my message went out to three million Christians, another event in my life confirming I am a mouthpiece for God. What an honor and privilege to be anointed with such a powerful gift.

CHAPTER 20

Let Your Senses Dance with Electrifying Energy

It is now 2015 and I am planning my next adventure to a new world. I travelled to Turkey in the fall. I stayed in Istanbul by myself for four days and then joined a group of travelers for a two-week tour of the country. It was a feast for the senses. The exquisite architecture of the mosques. The sounds of the Islamic chants were captivating. The *ezan*, or the call to prayer, is chanted six times a day, and you can first hear it as the sun is rising and you are opening your sleepy eyes.

The food delicacies gave off an aroma that made your mouth water with anticipation at enjoying a nutritious meal that totally fulfilled your appetite. The hustle and bustle of people rushing here and there. Cars beeping their horns through frustration. The chatter of merchants trying to close a deal so their families could eat that night. Is this a circus? A Broadway show? Or simply chaos with absolutely no order whatsoever?

I loved every step I took, I enjoyed the excitement of turning every corner; but most of all, I loved feeling alive.

We explored Istanbul, which is one of the largest cities in the world. Istanbul stretches across a narrow strait that connects Asia and Europe, making it the only city in the world spanning two continents. There are thirty million people that live in this city. In the old city, the most impressive historic sites were Hagia Sophia, Blue Mosque, and Topkapi Palace.

We visited Konya, one of the oldest cities in the world and best known for its remarkable Seljuk architecture and whirling dervishes. They are best known for their religious ceremonies in which they spin around and around on the left foot while wearing white billowing gowns. I was privileged to see one of their performances and it was spellbinding. It was so beautifully choreographed, synchronized, and one of the most breathtaking performances I have ever seen.

The next place was Cappadocia which is best known for its fairy-tale landscape of unusual formations resembling chimneys, cones, and pinnacles. Natural processes, such as ancient volcanic eruptions and erosion, have all sculpted these old formations over the years. Mankind added remarkable touches to the landscape by carving out houses, churches, and underground cities from the soft rock.

In the morning hours on awakening, I looked out of my bedroom window and saw over a hundred hot-air balloons drifting over the fairytale castles. It was so breathtaking that you had to wipe your eyes in disbelief at the surreal picture before you.

That morning, we all went for a balloon ride and saw the whole landscape of Cappadocia from a bird's-eye view. There are no words to describe the awesomeness of the whole experience.

Another highlight of the trip was visiting the world-famous ancient Greco-Roman site of Ephesus, one of the largest and best preserved ancient cities in the world and a UNESCO World Heritage Site. I walked on the remarkably preserved wide marble streets flanked by columns and temples. I saw the Library of Celsus, a tiered façade decorated with exquisite statues. The amphitheater is the one where St. Paul preached to the Ephesians. There were remarkably preserved baths. Ephesus was also the site of the Temple of Artemis, one of the Seven Wonders of the Ancient World.

Paul and the disciples only became fully convicted with their message of salvation and eternal life after Jesus Christ rose from the grave. Can you imagine living every day, after speaking to the crowds, knowing there was the possibility that you could die that day in some gruesome way? They all died tragically, except for John.

Turkey gave me a glimpse of what it was like living 2000 years ago. As I walked around Ephesus, my imagination let me hear the hustle and bustle of the marketplace. I imagined camels and sheep being herded to auction, the stench of animal droppings; nobility being carried around on carriages so their feet never had to step on the common ground; scholars leaving the library, carrying sacred books tucked securely under their arm, slaves beaten down by their masters' whipped, hungry, tired, and used to fulfill the pleasures of the rich; young women robbed of their virginity and their childlike spirit at a young age; the sound of running water flowing through the streets bringing a renewed energy to the children who wanted to run free.

Oh, how I love my free spirit which is not trapped in time and space. My living water comes from God who continually waters my garden.

The next day, it was time to say farewell to my fellow travelers and get on a plane to continue my travels for another adventure. I arrived in Prague late in the evening and booked into a local hotel. Prague is at the geographical heart of Europe. After I settled down in my room and took a small nap, I was ready to explore. I left my hotel and walked up the main road, not knowing where I was going. Suddenly, out of darkness of the night loomed tall buildings situated around an old town square. I stopped in my tracks and stood very still, slowly perusing the landscape. I saw two churches, a building with a clock on it, lots of street-sellers hawking their wares. There where people sitting at cafes, eating and drinking, merrily celebrating life.

I was hungry and found a small pizza parlor where I could sit quietly by myself and observe the mesmerizing commotion of the square. As I ate my pizza, all of a sudden, a violinist struck a cord and my whole being was transported to a magical place in time. I had goosebumps over every inch of my body. My eyes swelled up with uncontrollable emotion that came from the pit of my stomach. I was in ecstasy and never wanted the moment to end. I could not place the song the violinist was playing, but it seemed very familiar.

Over the next week, I visited several sites in Prague—the spectacular Gothic St. Vitus's Cathedral, St. Agnes's Convent, and Prague Castle where I witnessed the changing of the guard; the most captivating walk across Charles Bridge which was lined with thirty statues. The saints and other religious figures were installed from 1683 onwards to lead the masses back to mass.

I walked across the bridge around sunset and the clouds appeared three dimensional against the red sky. The shadows of the statues on the cobblestone path led your imagination to conjure up stories of ancient times like the story of John Nepomuk who was thrown off the bridge to his death. Did he scream with terror as he faced his death? Or did he willingly accept his fate? As I was walking across the bridge, the eyes of the statues followed me, watching my every move. They were so lifelike, I thought one may jump down and push me over the bridge and no one would ever know what had happened to me. I had not informed anyone back home where I was staying. Oh, Little Anne, what an amazing storyteller you are.

As I reached the end of the bridge, a violinist began playing the same song that I heard the first day I arrived in Prague. Suddenly it came to me. The song was called "The Secret Garden." I had played that song over and over again in my apartment back home. Why I did not immediately recognize the song, I have no idea. It was so hard to leave Prague, but I tucked all my memories away in my heart.

The next stop was the Philippines to help assist a workshop on self-empowerment. The airline flight was long and tiring, but I eventually arrived, suitcase in hand. I was met at the airport by the lady hosting the workshop.

The property where we stayed was surrounded by luscious tall trees, and the noises of the different birds were delightful.

The day of the workshop, about fifteen ladies attended. They were very excited and thrilled to meet Dorothy from Australia and myself from America. My part of the presentation was telling my story and then teaching skills on self-empowerment and enlightenment. I was very impressed with the ladies. They were so knowledgeable and had a much higher level of self-awareness than Americans. It was a pleasure and honor serving them.

I observed closely their reaction toward me. They immediately bonded with me, and there was a mutual trust between us which happened almost immediately before I spoke a word.

I loved their enquiring questions. They were very thought-provoking and, of course, my higher consciousness was working overtime. That's the way I like to work. Everyone is your teacher, and every day, I want to learn something new. That's the wonder of life when you follow your spirit and stay present in the moment.

At the end of the workshop, I was thankful to be going home to America. It was time to take my travelling shoes off and relax for a while. I needed to catch up on my sleep and reflect on my unforgettable travels.

CHAPTER 21

God's Plan for Your Life is Perfectly Crafted

I t is now the Spring of 2016. At this stage of my journey, I have had many conversations with God about my life's purpose. Although I knew God wanted me to write a book and be His eyes, ears, and mouth, I argued with Him continually, saying, "What can I possibly say that has not already been said?" There are millions of books on Christianity, self-awareness, living in the moment, the law of attraction, etc. I did not want to carry my cross because I could not see how I could possibly make a difference in the world. Most people I had worked with wanted what I had but were not willing to take the necessary action to change.

God, in His wisdom, always knows how to "set the stage" for an individual to be convinced that they must carry out their anointed service.

One of my Christian friends, Sadie, had a house in Tahoe. She invited four of us to go up and stay at her house for a few days. Sadie had mentioned about performing a Sozo session with me. To briefly explain this, it is when Jesus is invited into the room, and any underlying dramas or unresolved issues hopefully come to the surface and are released.

I knew without a doubt that this was exactly what God intended to happen during my stay in Tahoe. I always have the courage to follow through with God's direction. So around the second day, I encouraged Sadie to set up a time when we could conduct the session that evening. There were three of us in the room. Sadie would start the session with prayer, another person would write down exactly what would transpire, and I was just to sit still and wait for Sadie to invite Jesus into the room.

My heart was pounding, my hands were sweating, my whole body contorted with anxiety. What was going to happen? Was I going to embarrass myself in front of my friends? Well, there was no turning back now.

I closed my eyes and the process began. The first scene, I was walking hand in hand with Jesus down a country road. We were looking at each other, and Little Anne was so happy.

The next scene, I was at the Last Supper and I was seated to the far right of the table. I sensed the presence of someone sitting to my left, which after looking at the seating arrangement on the official site, I would have been sitting next to John. I was overcome with emotion because Jesus washed my feet first.

In the third vision, I was with Jesus in the garden of Gethsemane, and I stayed up all night with Him while He prayed. I remember how dark and eerie the scene was. The shadows of the trees seemed to stretch out, trying to consume us with darkness. I felt a feeling of entrapment, like I was doomed to be there forever.

When the soldiers came in the morning, I tried to defend Jesus by hitting them, but Jesus told me to stop. I was full of rage and anger that they wanted to arrest my Lord. I think I was screaming really loud, "No, no you cannot do that!"

In the next scene, I was helping Jesus carry his cross in the streets of Jerusalem. The path was dusty, dry, and the cries of the people were frightening. The walk seemed to last for hours. Jesus whispered to me, "You have to carry your cross, Anne, no matter what. The burden you will have to carry is nothing compared to what I am going through right now."

Next, Jesus was on the cross and His blood was dropping on my head. I was crying profusely. I felt so forlorn, but most of all, I felt hopeless and powerless over the situation. Two angels came and wrapped their wings around me, making me invisible to the guards.

After Jesus was taken down from the cross and laid in the tomb, I helped wrap his body with linen cloth. When everyone had left, I stepped into Jesus's body. It was like being immersed in a warm, peaceful, all-consuming energy. A place called home.

My Lord proceeded to cut off my nose, cut out my tongue, and cut off my ears and replaced them with new ones. He then held my heart and massaged it ever so slowly. He told me yet again, "You must carry your cross, Anne, only you can do the service God has anointed you with." He then told me to stand up, but I wouldn't. I wanted to stay inside His body with Him. He said, "I will never leave you, my child, I will help you on your journey."

So I eventually stepped out of His body. The stone covering the tomb moved aside and we both walked out together. Jesus looked at me and told me how much He loved me and not to be afraid. He then ascended up into the clouds.

After that encounter, I was fully committed to doing the service God had anointed me to do. I knew with all my heart that no matter what I had to face, God would love me, protect me, and guide me every step of the way.

When I opened my eyes, Sadie and her friend looked at each other in total astonishment. They said they had never witnessed anything like that before.

The trip to Tahoe was a success. My life had changed forever.

My next trip that year was to Croatia. I sailed on a riverboat from Zagreb, Croatia, to Athens along the Adriatic coast. The scenery was breathtaking. Some of the towns along the coast looked like a picture postcard.

One such town I visited was Hvar. It is a town with a unique cultural and historical heritage. It is famous for a unique kind of lace made from agave fibers handwoven by the Benedictine nuns. The nuns lived their entire lives indoors, making the exquisite pieces of art. No two pieces are the same.

My favorite town was Dubrovnik, surrounded by a wall which was built in the period from the twelfth to the second half of the seventeenth century. The main wall was 6400 feet long. As I walked around the castle walls, I enjoyed the views of the narrow streets and lively squares. I saw fortresses which defended Dubrovnik during battles in history. On the seaside section of the city walls, I enjoyed views of the crystal clear Adriatic Sea. The multicolored rooftops of the houses below were enchanting and breathtaking in structure.

I felt like I was in medieval times and imagined knights with javelins competing in battle, the adrenaline rush of the crowds anticipating the blood and gore of the defeated knight lying on the ground taking his last dying breath.

There were beautifully decorated boutiques enticing visitors to enter in to see their showcases displaying one of a kind merchandise. The cash register rang copious credit cards through their machines. The merchants smiled like a Cheshire cat, thinking of all the extra profits they were making.

I thoroughly enjoyed all the towns and islands we visited along the way. We travelled through Bosnia, Montenegro, Albania, and finished up in Athens, Greece.

Once I got to Athens, I had left my travelling companions and had booked a room at a hotel from a travel site in America. I could not believe how awful the room was. It was now time for prayer. *Please, God, help me find a hotel with a great view of Athens.* I had no phone to use to help me find alternative accommodations.

That morning, I went for a walk with a friend from the river cruise. Our destination was to find a very old church located high on a hill that overlooked the city. As we were walking up the cobbled paved road, I saw a beautiful hotel to the right of us.

I said to my friend, "Look at that luxurious hotel. I wonder if they have any open reservations."

My companion said, "You will never be able to afford that hotel."

I turned to him and said, "Oh really? I prayed this morning, God always delivers."

I went into the foyer of the hotel to the reception desk. I asked if they had any rooms available, and a lady with beautiful blonde hair and sparkling eyes said, "Yes, of course, how many nights do you require?"

I asked the price of the room. It was exactly the same price as the other hotel I was staying in. My friend was amazed.

The next day, I took a taxi from the old hotel to the new one. The receptionist handed me the key to the room, and off I went to see what my new accommodation looked like. I put the key in the door and opened it quickly. I stood there speechless. I think I dropped my purse. The room was immaculate! It had a queen bed with white and pink luxurious bedding. It had a Jacuzzi tub and lots of fluffy white towels.

Then I opened the double glass doors to the balcony. Oh my, oh my, I could see the Acropolis clearly and I had an almost 360 degree view of the city! *Magnifique!* My friend who came to see the room with me said, "There must be a God."

I could actually lie on my bed at night and see the Acropolis illuminated on the hill. *Heaven! I'm in heaven!*

I was fortunate enough to take a walk around the Acropolis at night and see the sun setting, a view to never be missed. When I was in Athens, God downloaded two beautiful pieces of "literature" which I will share with you now.

Life is a Miracle

Life is uncertain, mysterious, ever-changing, full of wonder and joy. Sometimes life can be fearful, unpredictable and unstable. But to live with God elevates one above worldly things. A spiritual life can ensure a constant loving presence, knowing that whatever happens, God will protect and guide your fragile soul.

Life is like the ocean, never still, always turning in one direction then another. Up and down and swirling round and round. Be still and listen and know your God, listen to His whisper, see Him in everything, knowing all of life was created by Him. Oh to dream of coming home, a place called heaven.

The cries of the homeless, who are faceless to the world, once they lay in the comfort of their mother's arms for a brief moment. There are many faces that walk this earth—the angry, the greedy, and the self-centered. The innocent children who once saw the wonder of a moment.

Emotions are folly. They distort the beauty of time. Mindful thinking is needed to overcome the ego, the destroyer of spiritual truth. Be brave, my friend, be courageous; life is not easy at times. God watches closely. He is magnificent in so many ways. Trust and have faith so you can live your destiny.

You were intended for greatness, for service to others. We are all connected, not separate or meant to be alone. Let down your masks and become authentic so you can teach others how to recognize the miracles in their lives.

Time changes all things, nothing ever stays the same. To long for the past is a tragedy, to look to the future is meaningless. A prayer can change everything, if you believe. You created your world, you attract what you are. Be careful. Fate is always knowing and keeps precise records of all your deeds. What you think will take form, no matter how much you try to control it.

A song comes to mind from *The Sound of Music*. "Nothing comes from nothing, nothing ever does, so I must have done something good." God in his mercy bestows me with unexpected miraculous gifts. The world may not approve of my free spirit, but God does. With my spirit comes imagination, spontaneity, courage, and child-like joy. The chains that once bound my heart are broken, the bird is free to fly to uncharted skies. Oh, the daily adventure is exciting and wondrous.

Many people have searched for the meaning of life. They thought great riches, prominent positions, worldly acclaim are surely the answer to the riddle. But alas, they search with amazing fortitude, only to want for more and never become satisfied. Oh, how foolish and cruel people can be in their need to feel complete.

Your soul always has the answer, but one cannot pause for one second to listen for direction. Surely my mind has the answer, not my heart and body that has natural intuition and discernment. One has to be open to change direction on a whim so the treasures can be found. But man likes routine, predictability, logic, and reason.

There is no logic in God's world; only trust will lead you to your divine purpose. How badly do you want to be on your path? Can you let go of self? If only for a while, and think of others. What a tragedy to not connect with the energy of nature, humanity, or to pray for peace on earth, goodwill to all men. Amen.

So, my friend, life is a miracle, don't let it pass by fleetingly. With the blink of an eye, it comes to an end. Have no regrets, no "should haves" or unfulfilled dreams. Don't let a tear fall from your eye with painful memories. Prayer can change your life spontaneously if it is honest and true. To not know oneself is ignorance. To claim to be blind is stupidity; grow up and don't expect the world to serve you.

Give love, and you receive love; forgive, and you will be forgiven. Sir Francis was a wise man whose poem has been read by millions, but how many have heeded his words? The energy needed to change one's perception is less than the energy needed to roam aimlessly around the world. Be wise and ask for guidance in all things. God is ever-present, ever-knowing, eager to fulfill your requests. The faith the size of a mustard seed is the only requirement. Can you or do you really want to know your divine destiny? Or will darkness consume your soul? Heaven on earth or hell on earth—you have a choice. But be warned, the slope is slippery, and continually crossing the wrong line can lead to permanent imprisonment, your wings become broken and cannot be repaired, and the walls will never come down.

> So as I say goodbye, I wish you well on finding the purpose to your life, a life full of the glory of God, your forgiveness through His son, Jesus Christ, His unfailing love, His protection, His faithfulness and guidance all the days of your life. Listen for His whisper and know you are His lost child who He wants to bring home.

And we all say *amen.* It's that piece of writing that's beautiful. I want to read it over and over again.

The next download from God is about fear. I have spent my lifetime getting out of fear and replacing it with the love of God. Love can set you free so you can become whole and pursue your dreams and ultimately make them your reality.

> ### Fear
> Everyone experiences fear at some point in their life, and unfortunately, some people experience it their whole lives. Usually, some sort of trauma brings on anxiety. If the experience is prolonged or is devastating enough, the person will remain alert, controlling, and unsettled the rest of their life. Fear is present when one feels threatened physically, emotionally, or sexually. It will cause a part of the brain to send chemicals to the body to cause a person to respond with fight, flight, or freeze. Once the body goes into the reactionary mode, a person cannot control the outcome. It feels the need to survive and will take immediate action.
>
> All this is not new information and probably understood by many. The question is, how does one overcome it? The first awareness that is needed is to identify if it is interfering with one's life, paralyzing one from decision making and living life on life's terms. Is a person manufacturing their own fear? Is it false evidence appearing real?

If one has a true desire to work on themselves, a change of perception can be accomplished with discipline, dedication, and perseverance. The world can be a peaceful place.

The biggest obstacle to change is the ego, the false self. It wants to control you, keeps you in chaos, tells you lies. Example, it may say, "You could never do that. You're stupid." One should ask oneself, "Is that true?" Katie Byron, a true spiritual teacher, has a formula of asking yourself certain questions to reveal the truth from the false in any given circumstance.

We are programmed to think change is work. We have to move out of our comfort zone. It is actually the opposite. We are moving into our natural state, because the body and spirit knows what is optimum for our well-being and life purpose. Again, fear of the unknown is an illusion, the egotistic mind wants to stay in control. The more peaceful you are living life, the less control the ego has in running the show.

God lets us have free will, but unfortunately, if we listen to self, we will always make the wrong decision. The mind always wants more. It is programmed to not be satisfied with the present circumstances. This goes back to the Garden of Eden. The serpent convinced Eve not to just be happy living in the garden, which provided everything she needed. She believed the lie that Satan baited her with. She falsely believed that she needed to have wisdom like God so she would have more control of her life. The serpent, which represents the Devil, convinced her to eat from the Forbidden Tree. The Devil will continually and relentlessly try to get you to disobey God. He wants us to make him our god. He appeals to the flesh which, when fed, provides immediate gratification. The seven deadly sins are not described as deadly for no reason. Sin eventually leads to death because we can never get enough, and so to indulge excessively leads to health issues and can result in death.

Pride is at the head of the list of the deadly sins. Everybody thinks they need to have status in the world. "Look what I have, I am better than you." The wise realize everything they are and everything they have is because of God. Humility is required to live right. Humility is usually learned from painful lessons in life.

I always say, "Remember where you came from. You could end up back there. So treat people the way you want to be treated, never make unnecessary enemies. You may one day need those people you supposedly left behind; or so you thought."

The whole of humanity is connected. What happens on the other side of the world affects the world with its aftereffects. There is no place to hide, although people think if it is not happening to them, they don't need to be concerned. Hence, the world is becoming more and more disconnected, no unity, even families do not communicate with each other anymore. At best, texting is the main channel of communication, where feelings and true emotions are no longer conveyed.

If you go back to the indigenous tribe of Australia, the aborigines, they had everything in perfect balance. They ate from the land, their bodies were muscular and lean with no excess fat. Men and women worked together, and no derogatory word was ever spoken to a woman. They would punish people for wrongdoings by shooting an arrow into their leg so they were crippled for life. They would make boats, eating utensils, and all necessary equipment was made from the wood of the trees.

How sad we have progressed to the state we live in now—obesity, especially in young children, wasted materials, pollution, overpopulation, hunger, poverty, and human trafficking, just to name a few. Some say, "If there was a God, He would not let this happen." No, if people had listened to God and followed His instructions, the world issues would be greatly reduced.

Oh, how ignorant and stubborn man can be! Do they really have the audacity to think they can do a better job at anything without God? They know better from reading the Bible the consequences of man who disobeyed God. But advice from the wise falls on deaf ears, and so the cycle continues. Our very existence is at stake, but only few care. Through world disasters, people are starting to band together, which hopefully is the beginning of a new spiritual and energetic change.

So how can you assess the value of a person's life? I believe that how a person changed the life of others is the main legacy one should strive for, having children and encouraging them to reach their dreams, no matter how small or great their contribution. The world is enriched with their very existence.

Love can change everything. It is what Jesus teaches. Love the Lord God with all your heart, soul, mind, and strength. Love thy neighbor as thyself. Love is what makes the world go round. All that is needed is self-awareness of others' needs and wants and acting appropriately with love and understanding. Loving unconditionally should be our ultimate goal. To work on oneself is the most selfless act one can do in their lifetime, because everyone they come in contact with benefits. A thoughtful word, a kind gesture, a smile, a word of encouragement, and someone who will listen can literally change another person's life.

Without fear, the possibilities are endless. Every dream can become a vision, and every vision can become reality if your will aligns with God's will. Become a spiritual warrior and change the world.

The safest place you can be is in God's will.

So it was now time to return home to California. I did not want to leave, but I had to go. They say, "All good things must come to an end." Goodbye, Athens, I will come back one day. I promise you that.

CHAPTER 22

Even When You Are in Pieces, God Can Put You Back Together

I t is now 2017, and I am talking to God about the qualities that are necessary for a good speaker. I had developed a somewhat judgmental attitude toward people who simply "will not help themselves." We are in such a crisis in the world that it is necessary for all of us, not some of us, to become enlightened and work together to save the whole of humanity. That, I told God, was an impossible task.

Again, God reminded me I am only responsible to plant the seeds, He does the rest. I am totally powerless over the outcome and should not even waste my energy predicting the future.

Early in the spring of 2017, I was taking a series of yoga classes in a winery of all places. It was a very peaceful place. During one of the meditative parts of the class, I asked God if He wanted me to go to Israel?

He replied, "No, I want you to go to India."

Oh no, I thought, *really?*

One of the indications that God is communicating with you is the sentences are clear, precise, and short. Sometimes the download of information comes from nowhere. I may be shopping for groceries, and all of a sudden, an inspirational thought immediately comes to mind. I am so secure in my relationship with God that no matter what He asks of me, I know I can do it. He is the power within me that helps me complete the task in hand.

People are fearful of having a relationship with God because they worry, "What will He make me do? Will I have to change? Will I become somebody I don't want to be?" The biggest stumbling block is, "Will I have to take responsibility for my actions and my life?" People don't want to do that.

If you don't hear anything other than this, God wants you to have the desires of your heart. That means, every direction He leads you will eventually take you to nirvana. The essential ingredient to follow your divine path is courage. Not many people are courageous. You will not get the gifts and blessings you want without demonstrating trust and faith in God. You have to step out of "your box."

Don't you want your own children to love you, trust you, and have faith in you? Didn't that involve developing a relationship between the two of you? It didn't happen overnight. It started from birth. Well, that's exactly the same with God. He is your father and you are His child. You must develop a relationship with Him.

Communicate with Him daily and spend time with Him. Pour your heart out to Him, understand His way of thinking. You will be amazed how kind, loving, and thoughtful He is, even in the small things. One step at a time. Don't try and rush the process.

I had travelled with the same travel agency for the last three years. For a single person travelling alone, they had excellent itineraries and were cost effective. Their trip to India was fully booked for the year. I looked around at other travel companies, but nothing compared to the previous agency I had used.

It was around May, when I was walking the dog, that I told God that there were no open reservations left for India with the travel agency I wanted to use. The sense I got was He didn't care about the details. That was my clue to reframe my question. "God, I will call the travel agency, and if they have had a cancellation in September, that will be the sign to move forward."

On returning to my apartment, I called the travel agency. They said ten minutes before I called, someone cancelled in September, the only time available to go to India in 2017. Well, it was a done deal. I booked the trip and I would be leaving the beginning of September. God is amazing.

However, my smile turned into a frown when I asked God why He wanted me to go to India.

He said, "You will be broken open."

Wow, that sounds painful.

I had a very long flight to take to India—fifteen hours then a two-hour break and another five-hour flight. Yes, travelling from America to anywhere in the world takes forever.

I booked into my hotel in Delhi and rested for the evening. The next day, we visited Old Delhi. We saw Raj Ghat, a beautiful serene monument where Mahatma Gandhi was cremated. We saw Jama Masjid, the largest mosque in India. Then we took a rickshaw ride through Old Delhi. Oh my goodness, riding on various rickshaws throughout the trip was the highlight of the whole vacation for me!

A rickshaw involves four people being pulled by a man peddling a bicycle. On the ride through Old Delhi, you get a taste of the authentic, the genuine, and the original India, the disorderliness of the streets, the traffic, and the pedestrians. The pungent smells and fragrances of the spices fill the air. You see buses, trucks, cars, bicycles, pedestrians, and cows all making their way down the same path. It is pure madness but exhilarating all at the same time.

We went to a local restaurant for lunch and they cooked the food right at our table. There was a buffet displaying all kinds of delicacies fit for a king; or queen, in my case. I love Indian food. Our server was a young Indian boy around twenty-three years old. He would smile at me continuously.

At the end of the meal, he took my hand and said, "Let's dance." He took me to where the band was playing. There were about six or seven of the waiters standing near the dance area.

I said, "What do you want me to do?"

The leader said to follow his moves. So the music began and I followed his moves exactly to a tee. Everyone was clapping, videotaping, and cameras were flashing. At the end of the dance, our tour guide bowed down before me. Everyone said it looked like I had practiced dancing with them before and wondered how I did it.

I said, "Have you ever taken Zumba? You just follow the teacher." I have to tell you I was so proud of myself. It was one of the most fun events during my vacation.

One of the most spectacular sites was the Taj Mahal. It was built by Shah Jahan from 1631 to 1653 to enshrine the remains of his Queen Mumtaz Mahal. It took 20,000 workers to build this incredible structure. The semi-translucent white marble is inlaid with thousands of semi-precious stones in beautiful patterns, and the building has four identical facades, a perfect exercise in symmetry.

I went on a safari ride through Ranthambore National Park looking for tigers. We saw several types of deer, owls, birds of every kind, wild pigs, but unfortunately, no tigers. We did, however, see tiger tracks the size of a tiger's paw. It was gigantic. The tour guide was so knowledgeable and told us so many amazing stories, we forgot about looking for the tiger.

I saw the tomb where Gandhi was buried and the original Bodhi tree where Buddha became enlightened. I saw Hindu temples built in the ninth and tenth century. The last stop was Varanasi, the spiritual capital of India.

In Varanasi, we saw the Thanksgiving Ceremony to Mother Ganges. We also witnessed the ceremonial cremating of family members. When the father dies, the eldest child has his head shaven, and after the body has burnt, he has to break open his father's skull. It is believed that if this is not done, the skull could be used for demon ceremonies.

There is a caste system in India. The Brahmins are the highest caste level in the traditional Hindu society. Historically, this caste is composed of people who by right of birth can serve as temple priests and scholars. The second level are Kshatriyas. They serve in public administration and government. Any job in public service is likely to be a part of this caste. The third level are Vaishya, which includes merchants, farmers, and craftsmen. The fourth level are called Shudra, and this includes laborers. Then there are the untouchables. These people traditionally perform jobs that are thought to pollute a person spiritually and physically. These activities might consist of disposing of human waste and slaughtering animals.

Now to describe the absolute unbearable, painful, and unimaginable conditions in which the people in the fourth caste system and the untouchables live. I never thought I would witness such horrific sights in this world. The number of children running around filthy, ill-kept, hungry, and terrified—they run around the streets begging for food and money. I witnessed a six-year-old child and a four-year-old child standing against a metal gate, paralyzed with fear, and the four-year-old girl was carrying a baby. The terror in their eyes made me cry uncontrollably. I saw human deformities that were so scary they could have been the scenes in horror movies. One man had a foot four times larger than the other. Another had a hole in his face which made it hard to recognize he was human.

Women would carry babies and beg for money, coming up to your car window and banging on it, the babies having been stolen from people and intoxicated with alcohol to keep them quiet.

There were men with limbs cut off, probably by the local mafia. They would scoot along the floor on their hands, trying to get from one point to another. The roads were lined with the homeless, hungry, and lost souls. Each day, they were hanging onto life by a thin thread. The overpopulation was a breeding ground for the most deadly diseases.

The air pollution was so bad, we were all coughing profusely, and some people in the group were up half the night with coughing episodes that lasted hours. So I can definitely tell you, with all sincerity, I was glad to leave India and have no plans to ever return.

I stopped off at Bali on my way back to America. What a beautiful place to stay! The hotel I stayed in had its own beach and five different restaurants and three different swimming pools. I would go to dinner each night to taste a different cuisine.

It is with sadness in my heart that the age of romance is dead. Couples who were sitting in the most romantic atmosphere you could imagine were on their cell phones. Either both people were on their phones, or just one while the other sat in silence. I witnessed no communication at all between the vacationers. What a sad world we live in, to not hear laughter and joy between married people.

The flight home was long and tiring. I could not wait to get home to my own bed. How wonderful it would be to sink into my warm cozy bed. I longed to be back in my old routine.

The first three days back in California involved unpacking, washing, and catching up on sleep. Then the unexplainable happened. I walked into my apartment, after grocery shopping, and could not recognize where I was. My apartment seemed unfamiliar. My eyesight was blurry and my body was full of anxiety. I felt nauseous and very light-headed. I had to immediately sit down or I would have fallen down. What was going on?

I felt out of control, unable to stop my racing thoughts, and went into fear; or should I say terror. I felt hopeless, helpless, and powerless over my situation. I called a friend and asked her to pray over me.

When I tried to sleep at night, old memories from years ago would come up and then dissipate. This went on for weeks. I went to see my doctor for an extensive examination. She ordered every imaginable blood test, but everything came back normal. She wanted to order an EEG because of my mental disorientation. I thought I caught some deadly disease in India.

I met with my sponsor several times, but she could not really help. I had difficulty driving and, on one occasion, ended up driving down a one-way street.

It finally dawned on me what God had told me. "I want you to go to India so you can be broken open." Yes, I had been broken open all right, to a point where I thought I would never be able to function again in this world.

During this time, I had two close friends who I was in contact with every day. I kept saying if God wanted me to go through this, He would get me to the other side. Benjamin experienced my most bizarre behavior. I had mood swings, uncontrollable shaking, and at one point tried to throw myself against the wall, hoping to fall and pass out. However, Benjamin had very quick reflexes and prevented that from happening.

This period of time was as hard as getting sober in 2006. I was at my wits end. I realized witnessing all the poverty and suffering in

India was the catalyst to activating my pain and "breaking me open." How much longer could I go on? I got no relief from the pain and anxiety in my heart.

One day I was in a store that I normally shop in and saw a lady I knew from the program. My first thought was, "She doesn't want to hear my story." Everyone I told about my dilemma thought I was cuckoo. However, I proceeded to walk up to her and shared my sad story.

She looked right at me and said, "That's exactly what happened to me when I came back from India."

Now I thought I must have misunderstood her and asked her to repeat what she just said.

"Yes, you heard me right, I had the same thing happen when I came back from India." She told me she could be in a store and all of a sudden not know where she was, start panicking, and began screaming for her husband.

I said, "That's exactly what happens to me!"

Because I am normally quite independent and used to taking care of myself, when this kind of thing happened, I felt like a defenseless child.

She proceeded to tell me she had to undergo brain scans to try to get to the bottom of things. All results were normal. She said, "Just go with it, it will not last. Enjoy being crazy."

Then the penny dropped. Why not? I was good at that. That intervention changed my whole outlook. It's amazing when you know you are not alone, your problems become minimal.

So I started dancing down the aisles in stores that were playing amazing music. No one ever noticed. The security camera probably had some great recordings. After ten weeks, God had removed my egotistic needs. I had no resentment or judgement in my heart toward people. I could talk to my ex-husband with a loving heart. I had compassion for people I previously judged as being broken and not helping themselves. Wow, thank you, God, for getting me to the other side.

Looking back, it was all worth it, but I would not want it repeated, thank you.

CHAPTER 23

Who is this Unimaginable, Amazing, and Undeniable God?

et's talk about *The Seven Aspects of God* by Emmett Fox, a new thought spiritual leader from the early twentieth century. I know some of you don't want to hear the word *God*, but unfortunately, time has run out. No more grace, no more hiding, no more making excuses for not doing your part. So there is only one thing that has been there from the beginning of time and will be there until eternity—God, who is faithful, loving, powerful, and ready to help us if only we ask. So I want to educate you on who God is and what He can do for you.

The first main aspect of God is life. Where God is, life is. When you walk and communicate with God on a daily basis, you experience unexplainable joy.

> For God giveth to a man that is good in his sight
> wisdom, knowledge, and joy. (Ecclesiastes 2:26)

The second main aspect of God is truth. Wherever there is truth, there is God; truth at all times and in all circumstances. This is a good test when you want to know if someone is from God. Do they speak the truth?

To know the truth about any condition heals it.
Jesus said, "And ye shall know the truth, and the
truth shall make you free." (John 8:32)

The third aspect of God is love. This is the most important one for us to practice. There is no condition that enough love will not heal. Where there is fear, there cannot be love.

God is love: and he that dwelleth in love dwelleth
in God, and God in him. (1 John 4:16)

Divine love never fails, but the important thing to realize is that divine love must radiate from your own heart.

The fourth main aspect of God is intelligence. When you clearly realize that this is an intelligent universe, it will make a major difference in your life. In an intelligent universe, there cannot be disharmony, because all ideas must work together for the common good.

The Bible says whatever you think, I am (God), that I will be to you. This means that if we attribute to God every quality of an infinite, intelligent, loving personality, God will be just that to you. That is why we say we have a personal relationship with God, unique to everyone.

The fifth main aspect of God is soul. Soul is that aspect of God by virtue of which He is able to individualize Himself. The word *individual* means undivided. So your real self, the Christ within, the spiritual man, or the divine spark, is an individualization of God. You are the presence of God at the point where you are in your life.

Jesus answered them, "Is it not written in your
law: 'I said, Ye are gods?'" (John 10:34)

When you realize you are one with God, the task becomes "our business" instead of "my business."

The sixth aspect of God is spirit. Spirit cannot be destroyed or damaged. It is the opposite of matter. You are spirit. Spirit cannot die and was never born. Your true self was never born and will never die. You are an eternal, divine, unchanging spirit in your true nature.

> God is a spirit: And they that worship Him must
> worship Him in spirit and in truth. (John 4:24)

The seventh main aspect of God is principle, and this is probably the one that is least understood. What does the word *principle* mean? The angles of any triangle add up to 180 degrees. This holds true to any kind of triangle; this principle holds. Principles were true a billion years ago and they will remain true in the future.

Prayer is answered because God is principle, eternally manifested in the same way. When we pray rightly, we bring ourselves into harmony with His law of being.

> Jesus Christ is the same yesterday, and today, and
> forever. (Hebrews 13:8)

Beauty is the perfect balance of life, truth, and love. In any true work of art, you will find these aspects are balanced. So hopefully, that information gave you a better understanding of who God is.

Now I would like to add what I consider necessary actions to stay connected to God and how to understand when spirit is communicating with you and not your own ego.

Firstly, this is a practice that takes years to perfect; it doesn't happen overnight. If this is something you want, you should be patient with the process. Everybody's journey is unique in the way God will communicate with you.

Spirit came to me when I was a child. I was at the bedroom window sad, lonely, and fearful. It is very important to be still, without interruptions, and listen. Acknowledge you sense a communication between yourself and God and that you don't just push it away, denying it never happened.

Wait patiently to see if anything transpires in your life to support the evidence that the information provided holds credence. This process could go on for quite a while until you connect divine direction with real life situations. I was told at ten years old I was going to a "far-off land;" that did not happen until I was twenty-three years old.

Once spirit has earned your trust, you will start praying and asking for guidance on a regular basis.

How do you know God is communicating with you? Usually, God's direction is the opposite of what you want. This is where the difficulty lies. "Should I trust this guiding light?" you will probably ask yourself. "Where will it take me? What will I have to do? I don't want to move out of my comfort zone, it may not be safe." Your ego's voice will become louder and louder. Remember, your ego wants to be in control of you. It doesn't want spirit to be in control, because then the ego will start to die.

When I was in my early thirties, I fought with God. I would pray and expect God to answer my prayers the way I wanted them answered. I wanted to still be in control of the outcome. This is where God is unable to give you or me the best outcome for a situation. Remember, we all have a broken inner child to some extent. This brokenness is the weak link where your ego and Satan will attack.

Satan's tactics are distraction, discouragement, delay, and doubt. He will put some kind of temptation in your way to distract you off your course, something that appeals to your flesh. Or he may say something like this: "You cannot do that, you're worthless." Or he may make you go into your head and overthink something so you talk yourself out of taking a certain action. Or he may say, "You know that's not true, you tried that before and it didn't work out, don't you remember?"

So what is the solution? Mindful thinking. When something negative enters your brain, stop that thought going anywhere. Have you ever noticed when you have one negative thought, you quickly have another negative thought and another?

Before you know it, you're caught in a downward spiral, and then your body gets involved in the form of anxiety. Then you want to reach for something to ease the discomfort. Maybe a cigarette, chocolate cake, or mindless TV. Whatever it is, most of the time, it will not be good for you, physically and emotionally. You go deeper down the rabbit hole. Then you simply cannot get out of the loop. So before all that happens, change a thought, change a feeling. You will save yourself a lot of wasted energy.

Something I have noticed some people do is pray to God and their prayers get answered, but they don't follow through. Don't do that if you want future prayers to be answered. Not recognizing, acknowledging, or being grateful for answered prayers is definitely not going to lead you on a spiritual path with God.

A quote from the Bible: "Be still and know I am God." That is the biggest challenge today—to be still. We are a nation stimulated by outside influences. The scariest thing is we don't know how to live any other way. Life is on the fast track and its getting faster and faster every year. People are rushing all around, trying to fit as much in their day as possible. They have unrealistic expectations of what they can accomplish in twenty-four hours. Scheduling your day and pacing yourself will not only allow yourself to complete tasks more efficiently but help you remain in a calmer state.

Why do you think people get cancer, have heart attacks, and die of strokes? It's called *stress*. Stress manifests in all kinds of weird and wonderful ways.

From my story, you can see how God has blessed me with gifts, blessings, and supernatural experiences. Why? Well, one of the things I do when God answers my prayer is do my "happy dance" and shout from the rooftops, "God is amazing! Do you know what He just did in my life?" I always give thanks to the Lord. I praise His name and always give Him the glory.

A friend of mine says, "Why are you so surprised God always answers your prayers?" The point is God is not required to answer my prayers. You should not become a greedy child at the Christmas tree wanting more. I get as excited today when my prayer is answered as I did twenty years ago. Remember, I am talking about spirituality here, not religion. There are many promises in the Bible that God faithfully answers.

Something I really want to impress on you is God answers prayers for the good of the whole. A good example of this is how God is downloading information for this book. Yes, my prayer was to write a book, which is something I wanted to do, but the end result is this book will benefit the whole. Anyone who buys this book will hopefully draw nearer to their own personal enlightenment and at least become more intrigued about this magnificent God.

After living almost two-thirds of my life, I wanted to help ease the pain of humanity. I wanted to help others to identify and become aware of their own road map that can lead them to heaven on earth. God loves this kind of dream if it is honest and sincere. Remember, we are all his children. God doesn't have grandchildren. So he will help you in all kinds of amazing ways to fulfill your destiny, because it is His will to have peace on Earth.

CHAPTER 24

Together, Let's Build a Brand-New World

Well, I have told my story, and hopefully you have had some awakenings to your own life journey. I can temporarily inspire you, I can temporarily make you reflect on your uniqueness, I can temporarily help you create a picture in your mind's eye. I can temporarily make you believe you want to be a part of building the new world.

However, this idea will not last. You will fantasize about being in love with the idea, but that will fade after a month or so. Why? Because the idea came from me. Anything that sustains life through the tough times, cultivates resilience through personal growth, and grows to fruition must come from you. You are the only one who can find the willingness, courage, and strength to persevere to the end.

After years of helping others, I am totally convinced I am powerless over people, places, and things. I feel the only way to help this world is by educating you on the choices available to you. I cannot tell you what to do or I will immediately get pushback. I cannot create your dreams for you, because I am not you. I cannot tell you the exact steps you must take to become the best version of yourself. I have no idea what resonates with you or what inspires you, because I am not you.

Why do you think people go to seminars for inspiration, read self-help books for personal growth, and join organizations where people can do their thinking for them? They believe they are doing something that will fill the "holes in their hearts" or make them better people. Wrong. The results are nil, nada, zip, zero.

People think doing these things bring them closer to their destiny. The thing that is always missing is authenticity and action. Few people ever walk their talk. Few people live in integrity. Few people will ever think of others before themselves. Few people will ever step out of their comfort zone.

People don't like change. They don't want to go through growing pains. They justify why they cannot take action right now in their lives. They don't want to be judged by others. They don't want to come out from behind their masks. Why? Because of fear. Fear prevents the crossing over from the old self to the new self. Courage is not the absence of fear; courage is facing the fear and walking through it.

So let me educate you on choices you can make that will change your life forever and the lives of people around you and, in turn, change the world, only if you choose to. You have the power of choice.

Every one of us is like the sculpture made by Michael Angelo. The masterpiece is within. We have to want to chip the unwanted material away.

"Why do I want to be the best version of me?" you may ask. "How will I feel? What will I have to do? Will it be painful? I would rather stay with the familiar, thank you," you say. That's your choice.

I know exactly how you feel. The world can look like a battlefield. You expend every ounce of energy just getting through today. Your boss demands high expectations of you. Your spouse is always complaining. Your children talk back and show no respect. No one hears you because everyone is on their cell phone or distracted by something. Your ego tells you, "No one really cares about you." Your false self says, "Nothing you do will make a difference," which is a lie.

Wrong, wrong, wrong. You have a divine purpose. Let me have your attention for the rest of this chapter, please.

So nothing changes if nothing changes. Correct? What if your life stayed exactly the way it is right now. Would you be happy? What if you bought a house, a new sports car, or won the lottery? How long would you be happy? Anything that is added to your life from the outside will not sustain happiness for a lifetime. Okay, you say, "But I just want to experience the prize. I deserve it." Maybe you do. However, every choice you make selfishly leads you off your chosen path. "But I don't care," you say, "I will deal with the consequences." Do you know what you are actually saying? Stop for a moment and think the chain of events through.

Let's take one example. They say money and power make the world go around. They also say that money is the root of all evil. When one of the deadly sins takes over, you no longer have logical thinking. I think we can agree that whatever decision you make in life, there is the yin and yang, the good and the bad. I think we can also agree that we have great expectations about the outcome of something that appeals to our egos. We don't listen to reason, logic, or other peoples' experiences with the outcome of such intoxicating things.

Pause for one moment and look back on your personal life. When you bought something, you thought it was going to change your world, right? Did it serve you in the long run? Did unforeseen consequences pop up that complicated things? If you say no, lucky you. Most people would say yes. Did it fulfill you? Did it bring you peace and a sense of accomplishment? Did you want more? Were you ever satisfied? Probably not.

One of the greatest tools I have personally held myself accountable to is a value system. It looks something like this:

List of Anne's Top Values:

Love
Intimacy
Health
Peace
Passion
Success
Adventure
Freedom

So when someone or something new shows up in my life, I ask myself, "Can I give and receive love in this situation?" If yes, next question. "Will this experience be superficial or have true meaning?" Next questions "Will this be healthy for me? Will I stay emotionally balanced? Will I be peaceful? Will this new event make me passionate about the undertaking? And will I be successful? Will this be fun and adventurous? And will I be free to be *me?*"

So having a value system allows you to align yourself with the true you. The more your body, mind, and soul are in sync with each other, the more peaceful, successful, and connected you will feel. So right now, pause and take a piece of paper and write down some of the values you want to live by.

Let's make this fun. Don't think too much. This is just a rough draft. Thinking brings your conscious thoughts to the surface. We want to access your subconscious thoughts. These thoughts are the true you. So the best way to access the subconscious is through journaling.

Now let me ask you something else. What do you think you are good at? Do you recognize some of your talents and gifts? Remember, we are focusing only on the positive attributes. Let's write some of them down.

I know, personally, I like to help people with personal struggles and want to share my wisdom. I am a good listener. I am open and honest. I am a leader, not a follower. I like attention and want to be seen. I am joyful and have a grateful heart. I am spontaneous and speak my truth. Jobs that would fit my personality and gifts are a writer, an inspirational speaker, rebel with a cause, teacher, and visionary.

This exercise may give you more clarity on the kind of career you are best suited for. This may also give you an awakening as to way you don't like your present job. Remember what the great sage said? "If you love what you do, you never have to work a day in your life." Of course, I realize sacrifices have to be made. You cannot always have what you want when you want it.

Something I know everyone has is some sort of inner barometer, some sense of right and wrong. Every time I ask a person, "Did you know you were making the wrong decision when you made that choice?" almost everyone says, "Oh yes, I knew better." I am not talking about people in a mind-altering state. So we are guided by something or someone. Would you agree to that statement? A simple yes or no will suffice. Do I dare ask you a more probing question? Could it be a power greater than yourself guiding you along your chosen path? It is definitely food for thought, don't you think?

So having read my book, you know I always listen to my inner voice, which I know is God guiding me. Did you notice He never lead me astray? God has never led me down a "no through" road. He has always answered my prayers. He has loved me even when I felt unworthy. He has been my teacher, father, confidant, director, and much more. God is worthy of our love, trust, and faith.

Let's recap some of the choices I have presented to you. Firstly, setting up a personal value system to guide you with decision making. Secondly, an awakening to what job best suits your personality. Thirdly, the awareness of an inner voice guiding you in the right direction. If you have difficulty doing this self-awareness, ask a close friend to help you. People looking at you from the outside can literally make you see yourself in a different light. We all have blind spots.

Now let's look at what the world reflects back at you. Do you see an angry world? Do you become fearful in certain circumstances? Do you see a hopeless world? Do you see an abundant world? Do you see a world full of opportunities? Do you see the best in others? Or are you judgmental of others?

What is reflected back at you is what is in you. This would be an exercise on self-reflection. If you see an angry world, what are you angry about? What caused you to be angry in the first place? You can talk this out with a close friend or spouse that knows your history. When I talk to Benjamin about challenges, hurts, what opportunities I should move forward on, I listen to myself talking. In most cases, I hear the solution and action I need to take without Benjamin's input. I simply needed to bring the situation into the sunlight of the spirit. Once something that has been causing you stress is talked about, the power it had over you suddenly disappears. You can access your executive brain and make a sound decision.

The alternative is to make decisions on emotions, and these are not giving you the true picture. Some people go to see therapists to uncover more evidence around traumatic events. However, it is important to seek advice for personal growth on a temporary basis. Therapists would like you to use them as a crutch so you cannot live without them. I am amazed how many people will see therapists for years and years and never progress. The therapist keeps getting paid, and you stay stuck. Be very careful who you choose to help you through painful experiences.

Remember, I am trying to empower you with skills that you can use to enable yourself to make your own choices and have control over your own life. You always have a choice.

Now, how about that monkey mind. What is it telling you? My thoughts used to drive me mad. Of course, every positive thought comes from spirit, and every negative thought comes from your ego. The ego is the false self. It wants to control you, and it does so through your thought process. It loves causing chaos and drama so you continually live in a state of fight, fright, or freeze. You live in a state of feeling unstable and insecure. You attach to people or things in an unhealthy way, trying to feel somewhat safe. However, it is all an illusion set up by your ego. You are not safe around toxic people.

From a spiritual point of view, it is the devil using strongholds, set up when you were a child, to keep you down. He doesn't want you to know you are powerful beyond belief. You may not even understand what the phrase "toxic people" means. It is people who don't have your best interests at heart. They secretly want something from you. They cause drama and chaos in your life.

One of the biggest awakenings for me during my journey to enlightenment was how much I gave my power away. I know I have brought this subject up before, but it is so important to know who you really are. So many of us walk around, telling ourselves false lies. Remember, the more we can live life in true reality, the more chance we have of being successful. I would like to refer you again to Katie Byron's work where you ask yourself, "Is that true?"

Where is it written down that we need to go to school, go to college, get married, buy a house, have children, get a well-paid job, save for retirement, and then make sure your funeral costs are covered by insurance? Society, our parents, and whoever else feels the need to control our lives. Hogwash! Enough! I want you to start questioning things. I want you to do your own investigation about yourself and the world we live in. Stop living vicariously through other people. Stop listening to the news and social media. Don't take anything you hear secondhand for the truth. Stop your stinking thinking; it smells as bad as it sounds.

I have studied people and noticed what things people respond to. They do not respond to commands, criticism, injustice, prejudice, and control. They do respond to love, openness, honesty, and caring. Everyone will flourish and grow if they feel seen, safe, and soothed. I know I do, and all humans have similar needs. We are more alike than different.

So I can honestly tell you that when you discover who you truly are, and this will take time, don't be hard on yourself. When you learn enlightening and empowering tools to maneuver through life. When you are free to be yourself without fear, the sky is the limit, but most of all, you experience self-love and freedom to be you.

Every person has goodness inside of them. Everyone wants to make a difference in someone else's life. Everyone wants to be a part of something. Everyone wants respect and love. Everyone wants to be a part of a community. Everyone wants to give and receive love. So don't let the world define who you are, how you should think, what you should buy, and how you should live your life.

So instead of saying we need to change who we are today, how about adding new ideas, new thoughts and new behaviors to our daily lives? Let the old toxic behaviors and habits fade away and the new ones take root and germinate. You have a choice.

Today is the day to take the first step to being a part of the community building a new world. All it takes is making a decision, a willingness to believe in yourself and that you are a very important part of the whole.

The question I want you to ask is, are you with me or not? Just be honest with yourself. Don't force yourself to do something your heart is not fully invested in.

The world needs you for its survival, but people who are not fully invested into something can sometimes do more harm than good.

I am educating you on self-discovery and putting you in charge of making your own choices and finding your own amazing discoveries. It's exciting, don't you think?

Now let's take a pause. Go make yourself a cup of tea or walk around the block and get some fresh air. Let the information from this chapter settle and resonate into your consciousness.

CHAPTER 25

Life is but a Dream

What is reality? Well, it certainly is not what the world would like you to believe. One of the ways our reality is distorted is by the news and social media. They are more concerned about ratings, drama which drives our ego, fear, and money. They are not concerned about giving us the truth. They want to control what we think, what we buy, and how we should live our lives. How sad. If the news, talk shows, and advertisements can drive our emotions, then they win.

That is how I used to live, and sad to say, most of the world today lives this way too. Somehow, when our emotions are energized, we feel alive. That is a complete lie. This leads to a life of delusion, false security, and definitely not a promising future. But how can the world think intelligently, with sound mind, and a sense of taking care of the whole when we are so self-centered and need immediate gratification?

What a dilemma. Millions of self-help books have been published. We have every imaginable speaker that can talk on every subject under the sun. We have carefully planned diet centers to lose weight. We have health food stores, but America has more overweight people than any other country. We have children going to school hungry. We have more homeless today. The rich get richer, and the poor get poorer. The middle class is disappearing. We live in fear more than ever before. There are more people addicted to substances than ever before.

There is more violence in America, and we have more people incarcerated than any other country. The elderly are forgotten. People don't know who their neighbors are. The list goes on and on.

What is the solution? The Centuries old search for enlightenment and peace continues. It is quite a dilemma. Because the world is always evolving and new values and behaviors are being formed, what is the truth? Our reality changes, but not really. It's all an illusion. That is why Mother Theresa said, "Life is a dream."

Let me humbly express to you some thoughts that I feel are necessary for a balanced, healthy, productive universe.

The Hidden Power of the 12 Universal Laws

When we choose to ignore the universal laws, we will experience struggle, resistance, unfulfilled destiny, pain, and lack of direction.

The 12 Universal Laws have been in existence for thousands of years. Their authenticity lies in the fact that they have been proven to be true over and over again through time.

For the new world to emerge, we must go back to basics. Back to what has proven to produce a healthy, balanced, and loving flow of energy and life.

The Law of Divine Oneness is the first law and it helps us to understand that in this world we live, everything is connected to everything else. Every thought, word, action, and belief of ours affects others and the universe around us, irrespective of whether the people are near or far away; in other words, beyond time and space.

The Law of Vibration states that everything in the universe vibrates, moves, and travels in circular patterns. The same principle of vibration in the physical world applies to our feelings, desires, thoughts, dreams, and will. Basically this is the reason why what others do or say affects us directly or indirectly.

The Law of Action must be applied in order for us to manifest things on earth. Therefore, we must engage in actions that support our words, feelings, visions, thoughts, dreams, and emotions.

The Law of Correspondence basically puts us in the driver's seat of our own lives. Our outer world is a direct reflection of our inner world; therefore, we need to accept responsibility for our own lives.

The Law of Attraction shows how we create the events, people, and things that come into our lives. All our thoughts, words, feelings, and actions give out energies which attract like energies. What you place your attention on is what you attract into your life.

The Law of Perpetual Transmutation of Energy is a powerful one. It states that we all have power within us to change any condition in our lives that we are not happy with.

The Law of Relativity states that each person will receive a series of situations or problems for the purpose of strengthening the "inner light" within us. No matter how bad we perceive our situations to be, there is always someone who is in a worse situation. Do not spend your time looking for happiness from the outside as it already lies within you.

The Law of Polarity states that everything is on a continuum and has an opposite. There has to be darkness so that we might appreciate the light. We have the ability to transform undesirable thoughts by focusing on the opposite thought thereby bringing the desired positive change.

The Law of Rhythm states that everything vibrates and moves to a certain rhythm. This rhythm establishes cycles, seasons, patterns, and stages of development.

Each cycle is a reflection of the regularity of God's universe. To master each rhythm, you must rise above any negative part of the cycle.

The Law of Gender states that everything has its masculine (yang) and feminine (yin) principles and that these are the basis for all creation in the universe. As spiritual beings, we must ensure that there is a balance between the masculine and feminine energies within us in order for us to become true co-creators with God.

So I know it will take some time for you to digest and process this information. But I would like to summarize some of the important points. The energy created by every negative thought, action, or behavior goes into the collective consciousness of the universe. This energy not only affects your energy field but the collective energy field worldwide.

The energy associated with fear is so contagious and spreads very quickly, affecting millions in a very small time span. The energies associated with the seven deadly sins—for example, anger—are toxic and can literally make people become sick. This can cause catastrophic illnesses, including cancer and strokes.

Have you ever felt joyful and full of joy and then all of a sudden you feel sad and lethargic? Chances are you met someone who was attacking you psychically. Some reasons a person may attack you are they are jealous of you. Your life is progressing forward while theirs is stagnant. They are envious of your looks, your career, your wife, or husband, or your environment. They are living in darkness.

Whatever the reason, this energy is not going to lead to a happy, fulfilling, energy-filled relationship. Now let's consider the ripple effect. That person's energy left you feeling tired and depleted of energy. You cannot effectively complete your daily to-do list, you start getting overwhelmed and stressed out. Then fear creeps in, and before long, you become paralyzed and immobile. Now that is just what one person's negative energy can do. Can you imagine what the negative energy from one million people, can do and the ripple effect? The contagious virus spreads as quickly as the flu.

Now think for a moment what we are doing to Mother Earth. We are destroying it through pollution, litter, and destroying plants and animals that keep the ecosystem in balance. Remember I mentioned we have an intelligent universe and there cannot be disharmony for the universe to work efficiently as a whole?

Simply stated, for the new world to emerge, it all starts with you. Yes, you can no longer avoid taking responsibility for your thoughts, behaviors, and actions. That's why they say one enlightened being can change the world.

I personally was motivated by a story I read on the internet a year ago. A ten-year-old girl was selling lemonade on the street where she lived for twenty-five cents. She had the intention of raising $25,000 for a charity. People told her she would never be able to raise that kind of money. She said, "Maybe not, but it all starts with me." If a ten-year-old can say that, surely writing my autobiography with God could potentially affect the lives of millions of people. I have to try and leave the results to God and the universal energy.

Remember, a dream leads to a vision, which leads to an idea, which leads to something being created. The creation is introduced into the universal energy. The energy is expanded, the ripple effect happens, and a shift in consciousness occurs. Remember, energy can never be destroyed. Where did the energy for the dream originate? In my case, from God. God is life, truth, and the way.

So the gigantic elephant sitting in your front room is starting to stink. What are you going to do about it? I know no one wants to be told what to do. In fact, most people will do the opposite of what you ask them to do, just out of mere spite. Ridiculous, don't you think? We say we love our children, our friends, and family, but that is some distorted truth we make up in our heads. If you truly loved someone, you would make a conscious effort to improve their life as best you could. People argue, "I don't know what I am doing, it's just the way I am." Really? No, everyone has some form of inner voice that brings thoughts to the surface. Thoughts that need to be explored and investigated.

Remember, the world is in crisis. The world as we know it will not continue to exist. God downloaded information about the future which I talked about in a previous chapter. It is now up to us to do something about it.

I believe we need to start with our present state of mind—all the good, bad, and the ugly—and add new enlightening and empowering tools to our present state of consciousness. If we are consistent, mindful, and diligent about this process, the brain chemistry in the brain will change, and a new revised, energetic, powerful self will emerge. I know this to be true from my own journey.

All the pain and energy it took to become this renewed, powerful, spiritual woman was all worth it. In knowing oneself, seeing the truth, and speaking your own truth comes freedom. Freedom to be you!

Thanks for staying committed to reading this book. I know you all have got to know me intimately and we have energetically become connected. The next chapter talks about taking the actions necessary to become engaged and contribute to building a new world. You have the power of choice, and choosing the right actions that resonate within you will be the right choice.

CHAPTER 26

You Have the Power Within You to Change the World

What an adventure we have been on! I am kind of sad the book is coming to an end. In this chapter, I want to talk about implementing a simple daily routine to help you start the journey to becoming the best version of you.

Most people think of themselves and having a problem, like the problem is an external feature of themselves. No, you and the problem are one. Once you change your internal belief system, the outside world responds to you differently and your problem goes away.

Whatever your story is in your head, it will be passed down to future generations. Do you want that? When we avoid ourselves, we contribute to the suffering of the world. Do you want that? Are you ready to manifest your awesomeness to the world? I know you are. Everyone wants to be seen, heard, and feel involved. You may deny it, but it is true. Everybody has goodness inside of them wanting to help others. Most of the time, we act like wounded frightened children, because that's what we are.

There are three parts to transformation: Expand, Explore, and Expel.

Expand

These exercises involve expanding the positive feelings in your heart.

Exercise 1: Look into the mirror each morning and set the intention for the day.

Example: I receive love, joy, and abundance from God and the universe in everything I do.

Exercise 2: While you are drinking your coffee in a morning or having your breakfast, write a gratitude list.

Example: I am grateful for my family and friends.
I am grateful for my life.
I am grateful for another day.
I am grateful for Mother Earth.

Exercise 3: Give at least five people today a hug and some words of appreciation.

Example: Hug your spouse, children, or a stranger, and say, "I am grateful to have you in my life;" or "Have a beautiful day."

Explore

This involves exploring what negative thoughts, false beliefs and sabotaging behaviors you may be experiencing and why.

Exercise 1: Turn your cell phone and TV off. Find a quiet peaceful place. Sit for fifteen minutes and notice what thoughts come and go. Notice any feelings in your body.

Do not judge what comes up, do not force anything. Accept what is and let thoughts and feelings just come and go. Let your whole body relax and enjoy this time to just be.

If you experience too much fear, stop and take three deep breaths. Breathe in for a count of four seconds, hold for a count of seven seconds, and exhale for the count of eight.

Example: Take a walk, call a friend, but do the exercise together. Take tiny steps, don't force yourself, tell yourself, "I am doing the best I can and that is okay." Start again the next day. Never give up, you can do it.

Exercise 2: Get a small notepad you can carry around with you. Write down when a thought arises. Then write down the feeling with the thought. Then write the action you take as a result of that feeling.

Example: Thought—My spouse did not say goodbye to me when he left for work.
Feeling—Hurt, sad, feeling ignored.
Action—Shut down, no communication with spouse

Do this exercise for two weeks and then explore any patterns that emerge. Question why you do that. How long have you been doing that behavior? Does it serve you? How do you feel after taking that action, following the thought and feeling? Do you experience low energy?

Suggestion: Change a thought, change a feeling, and change the action.

Reframe the situation:
Thought—My spouse did not say goodbye to me when he left for work; poor guy, he is so busy and stressed at work, he doesn't have time to stop and smell the roses.
Feeling—Empathy, Compassion.
Action—Do something extra special for him when he comes home from work tonight, maybe a foot massage.
See what happens when you don't take things personally? Most of the time, it's not about *you*.

Exercise 3: Name the things you don't have but want in life. Write them down on a piece of paper.

Example: I want a loving supportive community.
Financial Security.
Excellent health.

Post them on your bathroom mirror or on the refrigerator in the kitchen.

Expel

This involves releasing the new ideas, thoughts, behaviors, wants, and desires into the world. We want to experience balance, joy, and expel our light into the world.

Exercise 1: In the third exercise in the section "Explore," we made a list of all the things we want to include in our lives. Now we act as if all these things are actually true today. We repeat the sentences over and over again each day, several times a day. The brain doesn't know what is actually true. If you constantly say, "I love to serve others" on a repetitive basis over and over again, your brain chemistry will actually change and you will develop a servant's heart. What you believe becomes reality, because what a man thinks will eventually manifest on the outside.

Example: I love myself enough to speech my truth to others without fear.
I live an abundant life.
I make a difference in the world. I love to serve others.
I believe in myself enough to achieve my goals.
I am surrounded by people who love me and support my journey.
God is always loving me unconditionally.

Exercise 2: Visualization. Visualize and write down the world you want to live in. Now how do we all visualize the new world? We go within and listen to our inner voice.

Now this is my viewpoint on the matter of internal dialogue, but I don't think any pastor would agree with me. Your internal dialogue you experience with your heart and all your body is God communicating with you. I believe it is not necessary to be a Christian, part of a church, or read the Bible daily to encounter God. Probably no other Christian will tell you this.

God loves nonbelievers, the lost, the invisible, the mentally challenged, the incarcerated, etc. We are all his children and He loves us equally. He is always trying to call His children home. Yes, you heard me right, He has no favorites; we are all given equal opportunity to go to God and develop a life-changing union with him.

Now, if you want to be educated on Jesus, Bible teachings, and belong to a community of believers, then of course church is the place to go. But be careful, there are shame-based churches. These churches brainwash you into convincing you that you are a sinner and cannot live or survive without going to their church.

I was baptized on Easter Sunday in 2011, which means I was saved, forgiven of my sins through the blood of Jesus Christ, and given eternal life. It is at that point that the Holy Spirit enters your body and informs you of your divine purpose.

So what about all the conversations I had with God before that date? Everything He told me came to pass, everything He promised me, He fulfilled. He protected and guided me. So if He did that for me, He can do it for you.

So find a quiet space, turn all your electronics off, and go within. Daydream, wonder at life, ask yourself questions, and let yourself become one with the universe. Be still with your breath for fifteen to twenty minutes. I guarantee you one day, out of the blue, you will hear a small quiet whisper. Write down what is revealed to you. Keep a journal, share your information with trusted friends.

All people are actually very much alike. We think a lot about the same things. We actually all want to be a part of the new world. Deep inside, we don't like fear, lack of abundance, isolation, or the feeling of being unloved.

So now is the time for radical change. Remember what God told us about what would happen if we don't step out of our comfort zone? The world will end. Let's all make a commitment to Him. He is ready and willing to help if we just listen to Him, trust Him, and take the necessary action He instructs us to do.

Exercise 3: Be the change you want in the world. Become fearful warriors, equipped to deal with any adversity that comes your way. I guarantee you for the first time in your life, you will feel *energized, alive, powerful,* and *a part of changing the course of the history of mankind.* In other words, you will be living your *divine destiny.*

CHAPTER 27

Transform this World into an Awakened World Where we all Belong

We have had many events over the years of needless, senseless, and unbearable events where children and adults have lost their lives abruptly. This is a result of untreated mental illness in the world, and in certain individuals, the extreme buildup of psychotic energy in their brains has caused them to become suicidal or homicidal. We hear the news and we send our prayers out to the families of the deceased. The news shows us one photograph at a time of the dead victims. How do you feel? Sad? Fearful? What a tragedy, you say.

Now imagine they show the photographs of the dead children again one at a time, but this time, a photograph of your child appears. How do you feel now? Angry? Distraught? You probably feel like you need to take some action, scream, cry; but most of all, you have to do something about the situation. Bingo! This is my point. Even if your child is not a victim of needless violence, we must take action in the community where we live. Band together, set enough energy in motion to bring about change—change in our schools, change in our communities, change in our families.

We must think for ourselves, not go with the flow. Sometimes change is brought about by one person speaking up and giving another viewpoint. Look at all the great inventors of our time. If that person had not thought differently from the masses like Thomas Edison who invented electricity, where would we be today?

The earth as we know it is coming to an end. We have no choices available, only one choice—we must step out of our comfort zone, we must speak our truth, we must become aware of our present circumstances and not live in a bubble. Be true to yourself. Be courageous and lend a hand to a neighbor, a stranger and, most of all, love your own family members unconditionally. Children at school must stop bullying other students.

We are waiting for a miracle; be that miracle. Go deep inside of yourself and become the person you were intended to be. Don't make excuses for procrastination, don't justify why you cannot do something. Don't stay small because you are afraid what people will think. Let go of your story, stop being a victim, and become the hero. Do the necessary work to take off the veil of ignorance, denial, and see your true essence.

For our new world to transform, we must turn to a power greater than ourselves—God. He is all powerful, He can perform miracles, He is trustworthy, dependable, and wanting to help us; but we have to ask for His help. We need to listen to His direction and follow His instructions no matter what. Didn't my story demonstrate His power, His love, and His devotion to all His children? Now this doesn't mean not fighting or standing up for yourself. If you want a change in gun control, for example, you protest. You band together and become a voice that can be heard. Where God comes in is when your will is aligned with His; then He becomes the power behind your voice and makes change happen.

Stop trying to dismiss, justify, and defend yourself on why you shouldn't turn to God. The truth is if you don't want to accept God in your life, it is because you love your sin more and don't want to step out of your box and take responsibility for your life. Turning to God is receiving the freedom, love, and abundance you all want. Stop waiting for others to approve of your choices in life. No one knows you like you know you. Take the masks off and be your authentic self; that's when true transformation starts.

So in summary, let me highlight the most important practices that will forever improve your life, the people around and the world.

Live in the moment, be present and awake. God, nature, and the universe have life-changing messages to tell you. Always be grateful for everything in your life and give thanks out loud for even the small things. Don't waste your time on the petty things in life and don't have unreal expectations and assumptions of others. We have today and we will never be able to relive it. Make today count, don't waste it, live each day as if it's your last. Be aware of how your actions affect others. Stop thinking about yourself and your needs. Focus your attention on others. Random acts of service and ongoing committed services is how this world will transform. Remember what God told us what would happen to this world if we don't change our ways? We will not survive, time has run out, all hands on deck, or the boat sinks; the boat being the world.

Lastly, and the most important thing, is love. Take the necessary steps to love yourself, love your family and friends, and embrace the world with your love. Love makes the world go round, it makes people grow emotionally and spiritually. It stops people isolating and develops the need to connect with others. Love inspires people to fulfill their dreams. Love is what the soul longs for, a place called home. Love is not self-centered, judgmental, prideful, fearful, and all-encompassing. Love is kind and is peaceful in nature. Love can change the world.

God's love lives inside of me, and His light shines through me, and this attracts others to want the same. Love is God's beacon that says, "Come close, I will love you for you, you are my precious child. Come home."

I pray that you have all heard my message and are willing to become fearless warriors, banding together to build our new world; that your vision, passion, courage, and determination will never end now until eternity; that when you look back on your life, there are no "should haves" or "could haves." You lived your highest potential, you gave your very best in everything you did. That your light shines bright for everyone to see. You become the example of what a true warrior stands for. No matter what the odds are against you,

you believe in yourself. You know you are powerful and can manifest whatever you desire. I believe in you, I know you. Because I am you, and you are me; together, we are united; together, we are unstoppable.

Remember, there is a God, and we are never alone.

Amen.

ABOUT THE AUTHOR

Anne Hayes was born in England and came to America in 1983 at the age of twenty-three. She is an only child. All her life, she had to make decisions based on survival. She lived in the state of fight, flight, or freeze until she was in her late forties.

Anne believed what people said about her. She gave her power away, mainly to her parents and former husband. She lived a life based on conditional love. No matter how hard she tried, she could never fulfill what others expected of her.

Anne Hayes did not know who she was. She was afraid to speak her truth and she was a constant people pleaser and felt invisible and alone. Through all her sorrow, trials, and unfulfilled dreams, she came to trust and have faith in God. As a result, she has lived a supernatural, mystical, and undeniably blessed life.

In 2006, she should have died, but God, in His mercy and grace, rebuilt her life, piece by piece. Nothing happens by chance. God's timing is impeccable. Don't miss those life-changing events divinely sent to you; they may never happen again.

Today, Anne Hayes is a fearless spiritual warrior who is clothed with the armor of the Lord and ready to go into battle to save lost souls. She needs an army. Are you ready to join her?

With God by our side, who can stand against us?

Connect with me on Facebook at "I was never alone, Amen" for information on seminars and other upcoming events.